S0-CGS-062

ᴘPLOUGHSHARES

Spring 2011 • Vol. 37, No. 1

GUEST EDITOR
Colm Tóibín

EDITOR-IN-CHIEF
Ladette Randolph

MANAGING EDITOR
Andrea Drygas

FICTION EDITOR
Margot Livesey

POETRY EDITOR
John Skoyles

FOUNDING EDITOR
DeWitt Henry

FOUNDING PUBLISHER
Peter O'Malley

SENIOR READERS
Simeon Berry & Kate Flaherty

EDITORIAL ASSISTANTS
Sarah Banse & Abby Travis

COPY EDITOR
Carol Farash

ePUBLISHING CONSULTANT
John Rodzvilla

INTERN
Diana Filar

READERS
Akshay Ahuja | Chandra Asar | Jana Lee Balish | Rowan E. Beaird
Sean Campbell | Anne Champion | Adrienne Chan | Kirstin Chen | Joseph
Croscup | Lindsay D'Andrea | Ricky Davis | Jenn De Leon | Nicole DiCello
Aiden FitzGerald | Fabienne Francois | Keith Gaboury | Joshua Gartska
Taylor Gibbs | Kristine Greive | Daniel Gullet | Christopher Helmuth | Anna
Hofvander | Ethan Joella | Max Kaisler | Jocelyn Kerr | Eson Kim | Rachel Ko
Mary Kovaleski | Andrew Ladd | Jason Lapeze | Karen Lonzo | Valerie Maloof
Alexandria Marzano-Lesnevich | Jean Mattes | Autumn McClintock
Leslie McIntyre | Kathleen Merruzzi | Danielle Monroe | Nadia Moskop
Eileen Mullen | Katie Murphy | Casey Nobile | Chantal Notarstefano
Jennifer Olsen | June Rockefeller | Wesley Rothman | Linwood Rumney
Lindsay Sainlar | Nick Sansone | Shuchi Saraswat | Ellen Scheuermanan
Mallory Schwan | Kat Setzer | Ian Singleton | Brooks Sterrit | Sarah Stetson
Katherine Sticca | Sebastian Stockman | Jessica Survelas | Gina Tomain
Angela Voras-Hills | Nico Vreeland | Shannon Wagner | Caitlin Walls
Leah Welch | Caitlin White

ADVISORY BOARD
William H. Berman | Robert E. Courtemanche | DeWitt Henry
Alice Hoffman | Jacqueline Liebergott | Pam Painter
Janet Silver | Daniel Tobin | Marillyn Zacharis

Ploughshares, a journal of new writing, is guest-edited serially by prominent writers who explore different and personal visions, aesthetics, and literary circles. *Ploughshares* is published in April, August, and December at Emerson College, 120 Boylston Street, Boston, MA 02116-4624. Telephone: (617) 824-3757. Web address: pshares.org. E-mail: pshares@emerson.edu.

Advisory Editors: Sherman Alexie, Russell Banks, Andrea Barrett, Charles Baxter, Ann Beattie, Madison Smartt Bell, Anne Bernays, Frank Bidart, Amy Bloom, Robert Boswell, Henry Bromell, Rosellen Brown, Ron Carlson, James Carroll, David Daniel, Madeline DeFrees, Mark Doty, Rita Dove, Stuart Dybek, Cornelius Eady, Martín Espada, B. H. Fairchild, Carolyn Forché, Richard Ford, George Garrett, Lorrie Goldensohn, Mary Gordon, Jorie Graham, David Gullette, Marilyn Hacker, Donald Hall, Joy Harjo, Kathryn Harrison, Stratis Haviaras, Terrance Hayes, DeWitt Henry, Edward Hirsch, Jane Hirshfield, Tony Hoagland, Alice Hoffman, Fanny Howe, Marie Howe, Gish Jen, Justin Kaplan, Bill Knott, Yusef Komunyakaa, Maxine Kumin, Don Lee, Philip Levine, Margot Livesey, Thomas Lux, Gail Mazur, Campbell McGrath, Heather McHugh, James Alan McPherson, Sue Miller, Lorrie Moore, Paul Muldoon, Antonya Nelson, Jay Neugeboren, Howard Norman, Tim O'Brien, Joyce Peseroff, Carl Phillips, Jayne Anne Phillips, Robert Pinsky, Alberto Ríos, Lloyd Schwartz, Jim Shepard, Jane Shore, Charles Simic, Gary Soto, Elizabeth Spires, David St. John, Maura Stanton, Gerald Stern, Mark Strand, Elizabeth Strout, Christopher Tilghman, Richard Tillinghast, Chase Twichell, Jean Valentine, Fred Viebahn, Ellen Bryant Voigt, Dan Wakefield, Derek Walcott, Rosanna Warren, Alan Williamson, Eleanor Wilner, Tobias Wolff, C. D. Wright, Al Young, Kevin Young

Subscriptions (issn 0048-4474): $30 for one year (3 issues), $50 for two years (6 issues); $39 a year for institutions. Add $24 a year for international ($10 for Canada).

Upcoming: Fall 2011, a special 40th anniversary issue of poetry and prose edited by DeWitt Henry, will be published in August 2011. Winter 2011-12, a poetry and prose issue edited by Alice Hoffman, will be published in December 2011.

Submissions: Ploughshares has an updated reading period, as of June 1, 2010. The new reading period is from June 1 to January 15 (postmark and online dates). All submissions sent from January 16 to May 31 will be returned unread. Please see page 208 for editorial and submission policies, or visit our Web site: pshares.org/submit.

Back-issue, classroom-adoption, and bulk orders may be placed directly through *Ploughshares*. Microfilms of back issues may be obtained from University Microfilms. *Ploughshares* is also available as cd-rom and full-text products from ebsco, H. W. Wilson, JSTOR, ProQuest, and the Gale Group. Indexed in M.L.A. Bibliography, Humanities International Index, Book Review Index. Full publishers' index is online at pshares.org. The views and opinions expressed in this journal are solely those of the authors. All rights for individual works revert to the authors upon publication. *Ploughshares* receives support from the National Endowment for the Arts and the Massachusetts Cultural Council.

Retail distribution by Ingram Periodicals, Source Interlink, and Ubiquity. Printed in the U.S.A. by The Sheridan Press. Page composition and production by Quale Press.

Colm Tóibín photo by Phoebe Ling.

CONTENTS

Spring 2011

Cover: *The Spain Suites* 1, 2010. Acrylic on panel, 65 x 80 cm. Valerie Brennan.

PLOUGHSHARES PATRONS

This nonprofit publication would not be possible without the support of our readers and the generosity of the following individuals and organizations.

COUNCIL
Jacqueline Liebergott
Marillyn Zacharis

PATRONS
Eugenia Gladstone Vogel
Denice and Mel Cohen
Thomas E. Martin and Alice S. Hoffman
Dr. Jay A. Jackson and Dr. Mary Anne Jackson
Joanne Randall

FRIENDS
Christopher J. Palermo
William H. Berman

ORGANIZATIONS
Emerson College
Bank of America
Massachusetts Cultural Council
National Endowment for the Arts

Co-Publisher: $10,000 for two lifetime subscriptions and an acknowledgment page dedicated to the benefactor.

Council: $3,500 for two lifetime subscriptions and acknowledgment in the journal for three years.

Patron: $1,000 for a lifetime subscription and acknowledgment in the journal for two years.

Friend: $500 for acknowledgment in the journal for one year.

Ploughshares is proud to announce
The Alice Hoffman Prize for Fiction

~

*We're happy to announce a new fiction prize
from esteemed writer Alice Hoffman. The Alice
Hoffman Prize for Fiction will award $1,000 each
spring to a writer whose short story was published
in Ploughshares the previous year.*

COLM TÓIBÍN
Introduction

It was 1986 and I was staying with my brother in Omdurman close to Khartoum, where the White Nile and the Blue Nile meet. Omdurman was vast, the size of the city, but it was not a city in any way that I recognized. There were no wide streets or squares or municipal buildings, and services, such as electricity and running water and garbage collection, were rudimentary. There was a curfew, and the army was tensely visible in the streets. There were rumors of groups touring the city to break up private parties; they poured any alcohol they found down the drains.

Night fell in that world almost without warning, and there was something dense and magical about the last five minutes of unfolding light. In the often fading electric light, I listened to the BBC World Service until the sound of the radio, too, faded. Most people began to move around in the half-hour before dawn. The dawns were spectacular, the horizon a fierce pink and the sky a clear washed blue, the light sharp, piercing, exact.

My brother spoke Arabic so I had the news of the street translated for me. Neighbors were cheerful; there were many jokes. They called my brother motorbike because he had a motorbike; I was motorbike's brother. When I first arrived, my brother told me that one of the servants next door, a young man, had disappeared. No one knew where he went. My brother did not think he was abducted or anything like that, just that he had gone, perhaps he had found work elsewhere.

And one day he returned. When he said he had been to Nyala, everyone believed him. Nyala was in the south of Darfur; there was no road between Khartoum and there, just a thousand miles or so of desert. Trucks made the journey in convoy, but it was not easy and made less so by the drought. I had traveled a few hundred miles in that direction and it was tough going; there were dead animals everywhere and abandoned villages and dried-up wells.

And this guy had been there and back. Or so it seemed. He appeared to have done it on his own; he had no money and had no family there. For a while he was the street's prize subject of discussion. When he came to visit us, he was given tea. My brother and I sat down opposite him and my brother translated. "What was Nyala like?" my brother asked him.

The returned neighbor smiled and sipped his tea and thought for a minute. "Nyala," he said, "was *quoise.*"

"What was the journey like?" my brother asked.

The guy smiled again. "The journey," he said, "was *quoise.*"

He grinned in a sort of triumph. My brother explained to me that *quoise* meant "good," or "not too bad." The visitor continued to sip his tea; no question we asked him could elicit more than the word *quoise.* The people he met? The army? The villages? The desert? The truck drivers? All *quoise,* according to our visitor. Nothing else.

It struck me then that if everyone were like him, there would be no stories told, no stories written, no poems, no songs. It would all be *quoise.* All dull, left there, no glittering words or images to describe the real or imagined journey we are on, or have just taken.

It took me years to know better. Henry James described a colleague who wrote a much-praised work of fiction about the lives of French Protestant youths. When asked how she knew so much about the subject, she said simply that she was passing an open doorway in Paris once and she saw some of these youths. That was enough for her imagination, as James says, "to trace the implication of things." Our visitor that day in Omdurman, and the one word he used, should be enough for any writer. The look on his face, the silence around the word, stood for a great deal, left vast spaces for the imagination. From such strange curfewed roots, such reticences—a second of silence, a syllable of speech, a memory from 1985—poets and prose writers make a raid on the inarticulate; we take what we need when the time is right. What happens next is what matters.

JOHN BARGOWSKI
Sing-a-long

Just a few days before her final trip to the ER—
after she'd given up bingo and picking up her phone,

refused to get out of bed or leave her room,
living on a few spoons of broth and saltines

she'd crushed with the side of her curled fist
while they were still in their wrapper—

I signed in at the desk and caught a flutter from the corner
of the Activities Room where a jazz trio was swinging

through some '40s hits, my mother's hand in the air
waving me into the empty chair next to her

as she sang along with the band, the choir voice
she'd screamed away thirty years ago at my father's funeral

back again, strong enough that I could hear her over the crash
of the hi-hat and thump of the stand-up bass,

her fingers tapping the handrails of her wheelchair
in rhythm with the drummer's brushing,

me the silent one now as she sang the words to every tune,
stamping my foot and clapping along with the residents

when the band leader called it a wrap,
all of us begging for a little encore at the end of the set.

RABIH ALAMEDDINE
The Half-Wall

On a glorious, gilded Levantine morning, the day after the one-year anniversary of her husband's death, we heard the flapping of Auntie Lulu's strapless sandals climbing up the two flights of stairs to our landing. Glee and smile wrinkles overwhelmed my mother's face. She looked invigorated, as if she'd been dunked in an Italian fountain of joy.

Sitting next to my mother, our upstairs neighbor, Auntie Fadia, seemed surprised at first, then yelled at the half-wall, which was added to protect us from flying bullets that hadn't been around for quite a while, "Well done, my love. Well done. I'm proud of you." The half-walls, part of the post-civil-war renovation, were supposed to serve their defensive purpose while maintaining the building's older Beiruti character and keeping the common stairwell relatively open-aired. Like most things Lebanese, they arrived after the time when they were most needed had passed.

Auntie Fadia remained seated, fully coiffed as she was every morning and wearing a striped bright green muumuu. All the way from Hawaii, she'd insisted, even though she'd bought it from a basement shop that specialized in cheap clothing imported from Sri Lanka. She peeled a mandarin, using her long nails to pick at the strings of pith clinging to the fruit. My mother laid the newspaper down on the brass tray and poured a thick cup of Turkish coffee for her friend making the trek up the stairs. To my mother, pouring the morning coffee was a sacred ritual—irrigating the Garden, she called it. She placed the kettle atop the newspaper, fearing the ruffling breeze, and a porcelain saucer atop the kettle itself. She unhooked the clasp holding her toffee-colored hair (her latest annual color change) and raked unruly locks back into shape. In the domed conical cage behind her head, the trilling canary that had lost its voice hid behind a wilted lettuce leaf.

Auntie Lulu's cup waited on the brass tray. The stool she'd sat on since before I was born was right where it had always been. The three women had been having syrupy coffee together every morning for as long as I can remember, in thunder, lightning, or in rain. Auntie Lulu had sat on her stool a lot less frequently since her son Walid disappeared five years ago, and she hadn't used it at all in the last year.

Many of my earliest memories involve this landing, the women, and their coffee and cigarettes: twirling before them to model my first white dress; Walid and I sitting on the steps above, watching them gossip while we whispered our own tidbits about them; Auntie Fadia leaning her head back and unleashing her frightening trademark laugh, a crackling falsetto exhalation that made her elongated throat swell and undulate like a baker's bellows. My father would put his head out the door, the knot of his tie showing, but not the tail. He'd good-morning the women, joke with them, and shout down to Mr. Itani, Auntie Lulu's husband, to make sure he was ready for their walk to the American University, where they both taught. My mother taught there as well, but she drove her car and never rushed her coffee. She poked fun at her men because most days they walked in a dawdling mosey, and she picked them up along the way. "They want exercise," she'd say, "but not perspiration."

Auntie Lulu arrived on the landing. "What a pleasant surprise," she said when she saw me on the stairs. She smiled, which seemed like a herculean effort, as though her facial muscles had atrophied from lack of exercise. "Sit, sit, my daughter. No need for formalities." I couldn't imagine, and doubted she could, either, not standing up to greet her. I held on to her skeletal arms, and my nostrils inhaled a whiff of tobacco and deodorant. Her kiss felt like a Mediterranean fig impressing its texture upon my cheeks.

Auntie Lulu wore a blue scarf that didn't cover much of her hair and didn't match the burgundy blouse. She had but three scarves, all bought in halfhearted solidarity after her son's disappearance. She'd never worn them before. As obsessive as Walid became about our religion, he never once suggested modesty or propriety to any of the women in his life. It probably didn't enter his mind. His beliefs were an internal struggle against his failings. Or maybe he was just worried that any suggestion to cover up might prompt Auntie Fadia to take him over her knee as she'd done a few times when he was a child.

"I haven't seen you in so long," Auntie Lulu said.

It had only been three weeks since I'd seen her. In the last year she'd seldom left her apartment—a musty apartment that had furtive yet insistent dog smells but no dog. Auntie Fadia and my mother visited her daily, of course, and my mother insisted I accompany her at least once a month. I didn't think Auntie Lulu enjoyed my visits much. I was the madeleine of her failed dreams: I was Walid's best friend, and his brother's first girlfriend.

"How are your classes?"

I was taken aback, as was Auntie Fadia, whose mouth momentarily sagged. My mother straightened as if her stool had magically morphed into a high-backed chair. I had graduated three years earlier. Walid would have too, since we were the same age. My mother clearly wanted to say something, but Auntie Fadia was quicker. "Drink your coffee, my love." She handed Auntie Lulu half a mandarin.

I was the first to understand that Walid had disappeared. It wasn't a rational understanding by any means. It just hit me at the sushi boat restaurant, as if my soul understood first and my mind followed. Walid was a Heinlein fan (I couldn't stand him) and he loved the Martian word *grok*, which meant comprehending intimately and completely, understanding on a deeper, cellular level. I grokked that Walid was gone.

That December day began with mournful rain streaking my window. I was awakened by my mother asking if I knew why Walid hadn't come home the night before. He didn't show up for classes, either, and when I returned from university that afternoon, my mother dragged me to Auntie Lulu's for the first of many interrogations. As Auntie Lulu spoke, all I could concentrate on was her mouth, her lipstick having been applied quite unevenly. I tried to calm her and my mother. Walid was a man, a college sophomore, not a child. He probably wanted to spend the night studying or something, and then his cell phone battery died.

Yet when I sat down at the restaurant and saw the stupid connected boats going round and round endlessly, I began to weep. I felt so embarrassed that I ran outside and stood in the rain, heaving and choking on my tears, while being watched by a gaggle of parking valet boys huddled under an awning. I wasn't able to stop crying, so I didn't go back into the restaurant.

When we were younger, Walid used to fold an entire newspaper into squares and make cutouts, but instead of an accordion of little figures holding hands, his were a series of small boats coupled stem to stern.

I didn't know what had happened or where he was, but I knew he was gone. He had left his favorite jacket, a dark gray parka, hanging on the honeycomb wall-mounted coat rack in the foyer. Something strange must have happened for him not to take it with him.

Auntie Lulu hadn't moved his jacket, of course, hanging other coats around it. She went into the foyer every morning and kissed it. She must have done so this morning too.

Auntie Fadia lit two Marlboros in her mouth and passed one, rimmed with pale lipstick, to Auntie Lulu. "I'm so happy you're out of mourning," Auntie Fadia said. "A year is too much. I understand why you chose to do it for so long. I'm with you, my love. But I say six months—six months is more than enough. I loved my husband, everyone will vouch for that, but I couldn't keep wearing black."

"I didn't mind the black," Auntie Lulu said. "I just didn't want people to…" She stopped midsentence, midthought. She didn't look at us but stared at the half-wall before her. Had she looked above it, she'd have seen an unrelenting blue sheet of sky, and below it, our noisy Beiruti street.

"I think it's better that you took it off." My mother held her friend's hand. "He'd have wanted you to. Your husband hated black."

The three of us didn't need a map to understand that Auntie Lulu meant she didn't want to keep wearing black because people would think she was mourning her son as well. If she wore colors, he was still alive somewhere.

"And don't wear those black nylons anymore," Auntie Fadia said, leaning over. She put her hand on Auntie Lulu's knee but pulled it back, shaking her head. "Although they do cover a lot."

"Fadia!" my mother admonished.

"What? Don't look at me like that. I tell the truth, you know me. I think we could all use a little depilation. That's all I'm saying. Am I lying? Tell me. No, I most certainly am not. We all need a good pedicure as well, especially if we're going to wear our sandals. Am I right? Am I right? This evening we'll all go to the salon. Just the essentials, that's all. Top to bottom."

"Is that a good idea?" Auntie Lulu crushed her cigarette and reached for another from Auntie Fadia's pack. She hadn't brought her own.

"Yes, actually," my mother said, "it's an excellent idea. I certainly need it."

"And you know, my love," Auntie Fadia said, "unshaved legs are contagious. If we don't do something about yours, who knows what will happen to mine? It's even worse with unpedicured nails." She lifted her bare foot in the air and pointed at her scarlet toenails. "Look, look. The color is chipping as we speak. We need an emergency intervention."

In spite of herself, Auntie Lulu grinned. My mother laughed, and Auntie Fadia, who always enjoyed her own joke, laughed too. The crackling falsetto, the undulating throat.

"Girls night out," my mother said.

"We can be young again," Auntie Fadia added.

At sixty-two, Auntie Fadia was the eldest, and she wasn't aging gracefully. She fought every slight sign of decay with vigor and bitterness. Her makeup kept getting thicker and her fashions more adolescent. Even so, she looked younger and fresher than Auntie Lulu, ten years her junior, who was aging without bitterness and with obvious resignation. Her eyes had turned incurious a long time ago. Her elbows collected as many furrows as a walnut. She'd become a paltry imitation of what she once was. Her son's vanishing was a vampire. Fair was foul, and foul was fair.

Walid was born a week after I was. When they married, my parents moved into this building, which had been handed down to Auntie Fadia by her father. When Auntie Lulu discovered that she and my mother were in the same state and stage, she ascended the stairs with a stool and parked it in front of our apartment. They became fast and close friends.

I was my mother's first and only, and Walid was his mother's second and last. We attended the same kindergarten and the same grade school, and took the same classes at the university before he disappeared. Our friendship was taken for granted by all. He was my brother. In fact, when he caught his own brother kissing me in this same stairwell—

Tarek and I had stupidly thought that the half-wall would protect us from prying eyes—he broke in on us by yelling, "But she's your sister!" I was fourteen at the time and Tarek was older. He wasn't in any way family; at seventeen, he was almost another species.

Walid sat with me on the bus to our elementary school and on the way back. He walked at my side to our high school. He sat next to me in every class, during every lecture, and while we ate our watery lunches in the school cafeteria.

We read *Macbeth* for English class when we were sixteen. In our drafty classroom, huddling shoulder to shoulder, with flickering fluorescents and slanted sunbeams for light, we shared a raggedy, dog-eared copy. "When shall we three meet again, in thunder, lightning, or in rain?" A stampede of wildebeests or of militiamen couldn't have stopped our giggling in class on our first encounter with the three witches.

At home we sat on the stairs, our usual seats six steps above the coffee klatch, and when my mother demanded to know what we were laughing about, Walid recited the opening of *Macbeth*. My mother, the English professor, took up the second witch's lines: "When the hurlyburly's done, when the battle's lost and won."

Our mothers loved being called witches, but not Auntie Fadia, who declared that witches were ugly, as she most certainly wasn't.

"We are witches. Shakespeare didn't say they were ugly," my mother insisted as she poured her coven a second cup. "Try some of my witch's brew."

But two other mothers of students in the class objected, one a Sunni like us, the other a Maronite. Separately, they called our English teacher to register their horror at their offspring being taught about witches, which apparently was an insult to both Islam and Christianity. The English teacher instructed us to white-out the word *witches* and write in *weird sisters*. "In some folios," she said, "they were called the three weird sisters."

"I will not have it," my mother fumed when she found out. "This is a betrayal." Our English teacher had been her student only three years earlier. "You don't white-out Shakespeare. I'm going to have a talk with that ingrate. Capitulating to complaining idiots." She swallowed the hot coffee too quickly and coughed. "I am not a weird sister."

"Me neither," said Auntie Fadia. "Even a witch is better than a weird sister."

Walid didn't begin to be weird until college. He was normal—well, how normal is anyone?—and then somehow, as a freshman, when no one was looking, God crept into his life. As a teenager, he was as sex-obsessed as any Beiruti boy. He once forgot to log off a pornographic site, and when I sat down to use his computer, I was blasted with a picture of a man and woman in an unsustainable position. He rushed to turn the image off, apologized, and swore it was only curiosity that made him look. He wasn't averse to cussing or mischief. When we were thirteen, we pilfered two bottles of beer from his parents' fridge and pretended to enjoy them. Normal, he was a normal Lebanese boy.

Two streets away behind our building, there used to be a small copse of pine trees that was leveled to make room for upscale twin high rises five years ago. One day, Walid and I collected ripe pinecones, hid them in our pockets and underwear, and snuck up to the roof of our building. We tried to hit people with them and missed by a mile. We got in trouble, of course, and our punishment was spending the weekend confined to our rooms. It was terrible for both of us. He was normal.

He had the perfect Tintin collection, not one issue missing. It was the envy of his friends. I was startled to hear Auntie Lulu mention it this morning in connection with her daughter-in-law. "Tarek, may God forgive him, must have told his wife about it, and avaricious bitch that she is, she wants her hands on it."

"That ugly witch," declaimed Auntie Fadia.

"Hateful," my mother said, "just hateful."

"She went into his room."

"She did what?" cried Auntie Fadia. "That hyena doesn't deserve to live."

"She went into his room while I was in the kitchen and looked through his stuff. I was mortified. I wanted to scream, but all I could do was unleash tears in front of her. The worst part is that I had to pretend to be mollified by her fake kindness. She thinks I need to be stronger, face facts. Facts? She wants me to give his collection to my future grandchildren."

"And where are they?" my mother asked.

"Exactly." Auntie Lulu nodded her head energetically. "Exactly. Where are my grandchildren? Do you think I'm allowed to ask her? The last time I mentioned it, I got a talking-to from Tarek. I hurt her sensitive feelings."

"Hyenas don't have feeling," Auntie Fadia said. "Their laughter is only pretense."

"I can't bring up the subject of grandchildren because she's so sensitive, but she can when she wants something." Auntie Lulu paused, and just before her eyes went blank again she said, "And you, my girl, should have been the one to marry him."

"I'm afraid of heights," I said, regretting the words as soon as they left my throat. My mother glared with fiery disapproval. Auntie Fadia looked appalled; her eyebrows rose and thinned. Auntie Lulu looked oblivious and impassive. On her wrist, she wore a commemorative watch that her husband had given her for their engagement. It ticked no longer, keeping the static time of long ago.

Tarek was my boyfriend, if you could call him that, for barely a year, leaving me for pastures more svelte and ripe when he started college. In the time we were allegedly together, we never went further than kissing, and that only four or five times. We just liked the idea of discovery and the paradigm of dating. We had nothing in common. After all, the most original thought that had sprung from Tarek's mind, like a spring draft, was that he could wear a shirt that was darker than his tie and carry it off. He went and married a girl whose father was a war profiteer, a politician of course, and one of the richest men in Lebanon. For the wedding, the bride and her father arrived in a hot-air balloon. Even though the witches knew it was coming—the montgolfière, as the war profiteer was wont to call it—they were horrified as they watched the contraption approach. Had they had any magical powers, they'd have dispatched lightning bolts or a swarm of locusts and celebrated the balloon's plunge into the Mediterranean.

You would think that her son's marrying rich would have made Auntie Lulu happy. Tarek wanted to shower her with everything she'd ever desired.

"I want to move her into a nice apartment," he told me not too long ago as we sat in a gaudily decorated Mexican restaurant, a windowless basement with bright tropical colors reflected in floating cigarette smoke and motes. Even though we were sitting next to each other, he practically had to scream to be heard. Shakira Night was popular and loud. "Is that wrong of me? An apartment with a doorman and a maid's room would make life easier. She said she wouldn't know what to do with a maid. She just doesn't want to leave your mother."

"It's her home." I tried to drink my blended margarita as fast as I could. He was unbearable when I was sober.

"I think she doesn't want to move because she believes Walid will return one day," he said, "and if she isn't there, he won't know where to find her."

Gulp, slurp, gulp.

"She still thinks he'll come back." He sighed, took a sip of his own margarita. He was pale around his red-veined eyes.

I poured another from the pitcher. I knew what would come next. He'd been asking the same question ever since the vanishing.

"Do you think he got weird because of us, because of what he saw?"

I was still sober, so he was still pathetic. He wanted an explanation and I wanted to get drunk quickly without having a brain freeze. He was stuck in his desperate need to make sense of things, trying to believe that witnessing a brother kissing a girl could be a traumatic experience.

When Walid and his faith became intimate during his first year of college, he developed a few idiosyncrasies. He stopped shaving, but that wasn't much of a marker. He wasn't hirsute, and it took him quite a while to grow a beard, so he didn't exactly stop shaving as much as he never really began to. The disturbing tic, the real marker, was his sudden inability to look at a provocatively dressed woman. He didn't have a problem with me, of course, but if one of my friends turned up showing a bit of cleavage, his eyes fell to his shoelaces, gravity overwhelming his gaze. He didn't know how to respond if said friend talked to him. This was a boy who grew up adoring the cleavage Wonder Woman shared with Diana Prince. We had a French teacher in high school who wore a push-up bra that pushed up so effectively she could probably have stacked Racine's complete works on her bosom. Walid used to sit up front with a dopey grin on his face, his head swaying as if he were listening to a symphony and Madame Laffont's brassiere were the conductor's baton.

It wasn't one thing that changed him, one thing that could be explained. It wasn't childhood trauma, the World Trade Center bombing, the sight of his brother kissing me, the invasion of Iraq, charismatic clerics, excessive masturbation, or Israeli crimes.

Auntie Lulu rarely asked why Walid disappeared. She was more interested in where he was. She scoured every corner of Lebanon looking for him. She went to every police station in the country, literally, and forced the police to take her into every cell to make sure. She visited hospitals and morgues; held her breath and peeked under many a sheet. She secured the help of every sectarian party in her search. She made a high official of Hezbollah swear on the Koran that none of his people knew where her son was and that he'd inform her if the situation changed. She begged politicians subservient to Syria to tell her if her son had been abducted and thrown into one of its numerous secret prisons. She drove south to meet UNIFIL officers who might know whether the Israelis had kidnapped her son. She called on the imam her son had been studying with and made him feel so guilty that he tried desperately to help her locate Walid. He arranged a clandestine meeting with a crazy cleric who recruited fighters for Iraq—Auntie Lulu insisted she needed to hear his words directly—but the cleric didn't know anything, either. After a year of this, her husband pleaded with her to stop. She kept on going.

Auntie Fadia or my mother accompanied her on many of these excursions. After each one, my mother came back drained and frustrated. If I was home, no matter how tired she was, she'd interrogate me as if I were a disaffected citizen of her country. Did he tell me anything that might explain? Did he have friends that I hadn't told them about? Was I sworn to any secrets?

One day, some twenty-something months after his disappearance, Auntie Lulu stopped looking and began to wait. Waiting aged her. Waiting made her the woman who sat on our landing this morning, eyes averted, and said, "I saw him," another non sequitur. Her unmanicured fingernail scratched at an imaginary spot of dirt on her burgundy blouse. Out, out…

'"Who?" Auntie Fadia asked. "Who did you see?"

"I'm not crazy." Auntie Lulu wouldn't look up. "I saw Walid two days ago in his room. Don't freak out. I know it wasn't him. I'm not an imbecile. I knew it wasn't him even while I was seeing him. He was younger than when he left. I saw him. I talked to him. He disappeared again."

My mother reached out and hugged Auntie Lulu to her breast. I expected them to cry, but neither did. My mother scrunched her face in concern. Auntie Lulu allowed herself to be held, protected. Her shoulders slumped and relaxed.

As if to impress the surreal scene into our memory, a tinker led his mule-drawn cart along the busy street below, advertising his knife-sharpening services on a bullhorn. All four of us craned our necks to see beneath the half-wall. In a time long past, before the renovation, before the end of the civil war, before malls and French supermarkets, tradesmen traversed our street. The women of the neighborhood would call to them from balconies and stairwells. But now we were silent, as if studying a rare relic, a momentary, ephemeral glimmer of what once was.

About six months before Walid disappeared, I introduced him to Alex, a boy I was dating. Alex and I were at a coffee shop in the neighborhood when I saw Walid walking home and called to him. He was courteous, said his pleasure-to-meet-you-how-are-you, but when Alex extended his hand, Walid didn't shake it. Alex ignored the insult, either because he didn't consider it important or because he was dense. I couldn't. That evening, after his fourth prayer, I cornered Walid in his room and let him have it. He was thin, all skin and bones and flaring acne, and I wanted to press my thumbs through the saddle-shaped hollows of his collarbones until he submitted. I didn't allow him to stand up. He remained kneeling, the bed behind him, its sheets at low tide. How could he? I demanded. How could he be so inconsiderate to another person, to me, to someone I cared about? Was he now unable to touch a non-Muslim? Would shaking the hand of a Christian pollute his soul? He kept looking up at me with those embarrassed Arab eyes—desert, warm nights, vast and sorrowful. I wanted to pluck every single hair of that sad, inchoate peach fuzz on his chin. He would not repeat this performance, I swore. When he met Alex next, as I assured him he would, he was to shake his hand and not hurry home to wash, or

I would never speak to him again. I accused him of always smelling of moisturizing lotion and disinfectant. His eyes didn't leave me. He looked like a monk in a Zurbarán painting.

The second time they met, two evenings later, Walid rushed to shake Alex's hand. I felt guilty because Alex and I had been kissing in the car and his hand had ventured into virgin territory, returning with the faintest scent of meat and yeast and brine. When we got home, I told Walid he could wash his hands if he wanted. He said he could wait, his smile and eyes grasping for approval. He looked new to me.

In 2001, a few days after the planes were used as suicide missiles, the FBI or the CIA or some American agency released the names of nineteen men, one of whom was Lebanese, Ziad Jarrah. We were shocked, then horrified, then furious. He wasn't a murderer. He was like us. He was Sunni, middle-class, well educated, good family, nice guy. His mother went on television, his father, his uncle. They were secular, they said, and so was their boy. Like Walid and me, Ziad attended a French Catholic school. He had a girlfriend, his father insisted on television, a German girlfriend. He held up pictures of the couple for the camera, dancing in a nightclub, happy and not sober. His mother said he'd called her two days before the attack to tell her he was coming home for his cousin's wedding. He'd bought a new suit. He loved weddings. He was normal.

"Just because he's on the plane," my mother said at the time, "they think he's a terrorist."

His German girlfriend had talked to him three hours before the flight. He was pleasant and flirty. They were getting married. She had never met any of the other hijackers and had never heard her fiancé mention any of them. He'd never been to a mosque as far as she knew. He wasn't that way.

"Not just one of the hijackers," Auntie Fadia said, "but a pilot, and of course he was supposed to have flown the one plane that didn't reach its target. He crashed it. Incompetent terrorists, that's how they see the Lebanese."

We were angry. Why wasn't it possible for them to see the poor guy as a passenger? He was a victim as well. He was like us.

His mother cried on camera. "They don't know about us."

One of us, a grainy, somewhat pixilated picture, his school ID or driver's license, flickered in the top right corner of the television screen.

Not too long after, though, Bin Laden released a statement about the events, and he made sure to praise the martyrs, as he called them. He spoke of them in general but mentioned two names specifically: the Egyptian and the Lebanese, Ziad Jarrah.

I could only imagine what his mother must have felt when she heard her son's name on Bin Laden's lips.

Later, when a tape of the pilot making an announcement to the passengers of flight UA93 was released to the media, her remaining time on earth must have been shortened by half.

"This is your captain speaking," her son's voice said. "Would like you all to remain seated. There is a bomb on board …"

I asked Walid what he thought of Ziad Jarrah.

"I try hard not to think of him," he said, "or his poor mother."

My Walid was normal.

I could still hear the tinker's bullhorn down the street, but I could no longer see him or his mule. As the coven drank their coffee, I lit my first cigarette of the morning. I was trying to cut down. I didn't want to smoke as much as they did.

"I'll need to get my eyebrows done as well," Auntie Fadia said. "This evening will be good."

"I know he wasn't listening," Auntie Lulu said, "but I told him I'm saving his Tintins just in case." Her face remained expressionless as though it had been cast in wax.

My mother raised her eyes above the half-wall, to the section of the sky that could be seen, and sighed. She looked as if she were waiting for the heavens to crack open, for Gabriel, the trumpet-tongued angel, to explain the way of the world to her—the way of this impermanent world.

Like our family, the Itanis owned a small plot in a local graveyard, in which members of the family were supposed to be interred. Walid's place would be unused, probably as long as Auntie Lulu remained. I couldn't predict whether it would remain on hold after she left.

My spot was reserved, my own special Golgotha. I hadn't seen it, yet I knew where it was in principle, next to my parents and grandparents, to the left of my mother's. Would I insist on using it if I married?

Would I want to be buried next to my future husband? Would I keep my name?

The gravestone, upon its body, should begin to consider where my name would be inscribed.

DAVID BLAIR
My Philadelphia

Philadelphia can be called thicker—
home of W. C. Fields and Governor Rendell.
I've been flying barrier islands and the Jersey Shore
stretching to land in this place with some shoulders
and other padding. Has Philly sold out its paranoia? No,
it stayed thick, a thick knee, a thick elbow,
thick ribs, thick toes, thick color.
Even if you move from Philly, it helps to have
protection on you. There's some sort of reunion
of haters in a desolate part of the Philadelphia airport.
Some old wasps are sitting with their ancient
blond leather luggage and their faces show the marks
of a million whacks of a croquet mallet
or old tennis rackets with the names
of forgotten tennis pros, their crumpled sunhats
swirling like vermouth slickness. Who knows them?
Somebody is picking them up by baggage.
Remember the peroxide blond night clerk
got so bored with his hair at the hotel desk.
That was yesterday. That was Maryland.
But the high Walt Whitman Bridge
is a kind of armpit, and here a paranoid couple
of thick people are ripping each other's faces
off with kissing, heaving in their strands
of gold jewelry. Somebody else will come along
to end it all with some corresponding
greater thickness. Something unstoppable.
While the wallpaper ladies of Versailles might be looking
at butterflies, the oldsters sit like hallway phones.
If nothing else, we all have deaths on the line,

and nobody wants to pick anyone up
by these airfields that are whitened concrete
cemeteries where the sun finally husks
its own burial in blond, spent charcoal.

EAVAN BOLAND
Art of Empire

If no one in my family ever spoke of it,
if no one handed down
what it was to be born to power
and married in a poor country.

If no one wanted to remember
the noise of the redcoats cantering
in lanes bleached with apple flowers
on an April morning.

If no one ever mentioned how a woman was,
what she did,
what she never did again,
when she lived in a dying Empire.

If what was not said was never seen
If what was never seen could not be known
think of this as the only way
an empire could recede—

taking its laws, its horses, and its lordly all,
leaving a single art to be learned,
and one that required
neither a silversmith nor a glassblower

but a woman skilled in the sort of silence
that lets her stitch shadow flowers
into linen with pastel silks
and never look up

to remark on or remember why it is
the bird in her blackwork is warning her:
not a word not a word
not a word not a word.

Banner Creek Summit

It was Whitney Putnam's first time inside the Boise Airport. He stood in the baggage claim watching two suitcases and a car seat rotate on the carousel. The plane arriving from Denver landed twenty minutes ago, and the passengers have come and gone already. He searched the faces of women descending the escalator at the far end of the lobby, and he thought it was a conspiracy, the way they all looked the same. It had only been six weeks, but he worried he wouldn't recognize Emma Lee.

He took the stairs to the second floor and stood near the security checkpoint. The partition was a glass wall designed in the likeness of a river, and he watched through the watery divide as a man took off his shoes and emptied his pockets. Whitney knew nothing of commercial airports, could only imagine the experience as he'd seen it in movies. The flights he'd taken were in Forest Service helicopters, or the Cessna 206 they used to fly hunters into the Frank Church Wilderness.

Emma Lee O'Connell left the women's restroom with a fistful of tissues. Her face was flushed, legs weak beneath her. She slung her backpack over one shoulder as she walked the arrivals terminal, pausing to glance at her reflection as she passed a row of windows. It surprised her, as it did lately, to see she hadn't changed as much as she felt. A girl pushing an empty stroller ran by, then the girl's mother, laughing, calling for the girl to slow down, and Emma Lee told herself that coming home was the right decision.

From the top of the escalator, she watched Whitney pace the baggage claim. She knew him by his bowlegged walk, his restless hands, the chewing tobacco-ring worn into the back pocket of his jeans. He wore a dirty baseball cap and a brown Carhartt jacket. She wasn't close enough to see, but she knew his hiking boots were stained black with blood.

Emma Lee waved and Whitney waved back. He'd already removed the two suitcases, and the car seat looked abandoned on the silver panels of the carousel. She gestured toward it, and he looked over his shoulder. The car seat was white with a pink zebra-print cover, and he'd hoped it belonged to someone else. He struggled to imagine such a thing strapped to the bench seat of his truck.

"Betsy gave it to me," she said. "I got half a suitcase of baby clothes too."

They hugged. Whitney kissed the top of her head, just as her father did, and Emma Lee felt a part of her girlhood return for the second time that day, second to the moment the plane lowered over the familiar foothills of Southern Idaho.

Whitney lifted the backpack from her shoulder. It was busting at the seams with hand-me-downs from her cousin Betsy, but Emma Lee couldn't bring herself to wear the empire shirts or elastic-waist pants. She wore instead a new purple sweatshirt she'd bought at the airport gift shop, a Rockies sweatshirt, though she had never seen them play. It was two sizes too big and she buried both hands in the enormous front pocket.

Whitney touched her stomach gently, quickly, as if it were hot. "How you doing?" he said. "You feeling OK?"

"Better now that I got two feet on the ground. All that turbulence about makes me sick."

He motioned toward the truck in the no-parking zone outside the airport's sliding glass doors. Emma Lee put on her coat, and they walked together, stopping twice to rearrange the stack of luggage because Whitney refused to let her carry anything. He opened the truck door and she climbed in. He was surprised by the ease with which she moved, as yet unencumbered by the baby, and he wondered how much she was showing now that she was five months.

He lugged the car seat and two suitcases to the back of the truck and paused at the tailgate. The sky was a thickly knit blanket from the valley's wood smoke inversion. It was November, wetter and colder than any Whitney could remember, and he knew they should take the long way around—through Craters of the Moon—but he wasn't afraid of a little snow. He covered Emma Lee's suitcases with a blue tarp, then stood in the truck bed staring down at the car seat. It was already covered in plastic from the flight, and he thought at the last minute that he'd better weigh it down to keep it from blowing away.

Inside the truck, Emma Lee breathed into her hands. Whitney was sweating in his jacket, but he upped the heater. "I know you're not feeling good," he said, "but I need to eat something before we hit the road. There's some elk jerky in my pack, if the smell don't make you sick."

She handed him a piece of peppered jerky from a Ziploc bag. "I'm done being sick because of the baby. It's the flying that does it to me." She looked out the window at the gray belly of a plane. "I think it's the most unnatural thing in the world," she said, "moving that fast."

Whitney merged into traffic and they drove down Vista Hill. Below, the city rose up against a backdrop of white foothills and gray sky. It was after two o'clock, but it didn't look like any hour, just the endless color of winter, and it put Emma Lee in the mood to sleep. She looked back at the row of airport motels. "We're getting an awfully late start," she said. "Maybe we should stay the night."

Whitney drove on. "Whit," she said. "Did you hear me?"

"What's that?" He patted her knee. "Did you say something, honey?"

"Nothing," she said.

They crossed the Boise River and she read the sign for Julia Davis Park, then the Egyptian Theater marquee. She studied the outfits of women crossing the street, their black pea coats and colored scarves, and she tried to imagine what it might be like to live in the city. She thought maybe she could do it, so long as she didn't have to drive.

"It's sure good to be back," she said. "My cousin has a little terrier that licked my face every morning. It made me miss Roscoe. How's he doing?"

"He's still a dog."

"I hope my mother isn't feeding him table scraps. They say chicken bones aren't good for dogs." She covered her mouth in a yawn. "Betsy and John don't go to sleep until midnight. Can you believe that? I was sleeping on the pullout sofa."

"You must be tired," he said, because he didn't feel like talking. "Why don't you try and get some sleep?"

They had only been driving ten minutes, but already Whitney wanted to return to the quiet. His mind was back on the Bighorn Crags, on what had happened the week before while he was elk hunting. It was the reason he'd come for Emma Lee instead of sending her mother. He needed to see her, to know she was OK, and now that he had, he wanted to be alone again.

Two hours later Emma Lee murmured in sleep. Whitney glanced at her body slumped against the doorframe, then out the passenger window. Below, the Payette River snaked through the canyon, its waters laced in slush ice. Whitney tightened his grip on the steering wheel, as if willing the tires to better grip the road. The five-hour drive home was about to become six or seven now that it was snowing.

He drove the truck slowly up Banner Creek Summit. It was a road marked by light winter travel and heavy snowfall. Already the snow berms stood four feet high, and six inches of new snow covered the road. It was the time of day when deer and elk darted across, and Whitney knew the cold weather brought the herds into the valley fields to feed and bed. He'd worked the last two months as a hunting guide for a small outfitter, and just that morning he'd been fired. He was twenty-three years old. In years past he'd worked seasonally as a sawyer on a Forest Service crew, coasting through winters on unemployment, but now he had Emma Lee and the baby to think about. It was all he could do to think of anything else.

The tires spun, spitting snow, and Whitney let up on the gas. He pulled to the side with the thought of a new truck grill or fender, with the thought of putting Emma Lee in harm's way. He clicked the hazards and footed the emergency brake. Emma Lee sat up.

"Just putting it in four-wheel," he said. "You get some sleep?"

"Some," she said in a yawn.

He opened the door, snow blowing inside the cab, and closed it again. He fished beneath the seat for his gloves, patted his pockets, lowered the sun visor. An expired insurance card and a stack of receipts fluttered down. Emma Lee opened the glove compartment and handed Whitney two pairs: the fingerless and the rawhides. He waited for her to say what she always said—that she didn't know how he functioned before she came along.

"One or both?" she said, and Whitney took them both.

He put on the gloves and pointed to the highway pullout. A Forest Service outhouse stood at the far end. The snow was knee-deep, drifts blown deeper in places. "I'd park you closer," he said, "but I don't know if I could get back out."

"I don't have to go yet," she said.

"You might wanna try. I don't know when I can stop again."

Emma Lee shifted in the seat. She slipped her hand beneath her sweatshirt and rested it on the warmth of her belly. She meant to say, You sound like a father, but what she said was, "You sound like my father."

"I'm not trying to sound like nobody," Whitney said. "I'm just saying this might be a good time to go to the bathroom."

She looked at the brown shack, at the twenty yards between the warm truck and the cold toilet seat.

"I'll go with you," Whitney said.

"No," she said. "I'll wait."

Whitney said OK with a head nod. If he'd learned anything over the last five months, it was not to argue with a pregnant woman.

Emma Lee unfastened her seatbelt and leaned over. "Here," she said. She buttoned his jacket to his chin. Her hands were soft and cold on his neck. There was a time when Whitney would have kissed her hands as she did this, but now he didn't know how to touch her. He thanked her, and though he didn't mean it, he said, "I don't know how I managed without you."

Emma Lee collected the fallen receipts from the floorboard, organizing them by date. She didn't look up when she said, "I don't know, either."

Waves of snow washed over the windshield, wet snow that was crusted in ice. Whitney looked at the dash for the time. They had a half-hour of daylight to crest the summit. He rubbed an opening in the foggy glass and searched the road ahead. They hadn't passed a snowplow for two hours. This was the avalanche corridor—a thirteen-mile stretch that averaged three avalanches a year. Any day now the pass would close and stay closed until spring, diverting traffic across the high desert wasteland of Craters of the Moon.

Emma Lee shivered, more from mood than cold. She said, "Whit, maybe you ought to put the chains on too."

Whitney breathed into his jacket to warm the fabric against his face. He said, "Yeah, maybe so," and he opened the door and ducked into the storm.

He held his arm to the wind, walked squint-eyed to the back of the truck and lowered the tailgate. He climbed into the bed and rummaged through the toolbox. Emma Lee's two suitcases were covered in snow, bits of the blue tarp showing through like tiny lagoons. The chains weren't in the toolbox, and Whitney had to think before he remembered putting them in the car seat to weigh it down. He gathered the two sets, first in his hands, and then in the cradle of his arm because he kept dropping one or the other.

It took him five minutes. He rotated the turntable on the two front hubs to lock the four-wheel, then laid the chains in front of the tires. He tapped the side of the truck two times, and Emma Lee slid into the driver's seat and drove forward until he raised his arm. He loosened his Leatherman and used the pliers to secure the chains. They were too long, and he tied up the extra length with bailing wire to keep it from knocking against the fender wells. He worked awkwardly with his leg out straight in front of him. A year ago he'd torn his ACL, and now his knee ached in the cold. He thought about taking a painkiller but hated the way it made him feel disconnected and unsure. Already it was difficult to know who he was, and in that way it was becoming harder to communicate with Emma Lee.

Every night for the last six weeks he'd called Emma Lee at her cousin's house in Denver, and every night he told her he wanted her back. Whether or not that was true, he didn't know. He wiped his eyes with the back of his glove and looked into the dense brocade of pines. He felt the burden of the snow-heavy boughs, felt the days accumulating in a swift and dangerous way, and he told himself he loved Emma Lee and that was all that mattered. He brushed snow from the taillights, and the wind blew exhaust in his face, warm and suffocating. No, he thought, love wasn't enough.

The wipers fanned slow, wet strides across the windshield. Whitney knocked on the glass for Emma Lee to turn them off. She did—an unspoken language he credited less to their communication and more to their shared upbringing. He slid the blades between his fingers to clear the ice, then stood on the other side trying to look inside at her, to see in Emma Lee's face some recognition of the man he hoped he was, but she was heads down, her lips moving, counting.

Inside the truck, Emma Lee sorted the receipts, adding the sums in her head. She wasn't sure what she expected to find, but at the very least she hoped to piece together Whitney's life over the last six weeks without her. He was a man of few words, to Emma Lee or anyone for that matter. He hated to talk on the phone, was taciturn in the mornings and before bed, and although it seemed impossible, he'd grown even more private since she became pregnant. When she told her mother about the nights Whitney didn't come home, her mother laid her hands in her lap and asked Emma Lee, Do you want a family or not? Her mother said that in every relationship one partner loves the other more, one less. She said it was best that Emma Lee understand her place and try not to fight it.

Emma Lee separated the receipts into two stacks. She stowed the grocery and fuel receipts in the glove compartment, then pocketed the yellow charge slips from the North Fork Diner. Whitney opened the door. He tapped his boots against the running board, took off his gloves and wrung his hands.

"Hell," he said. "I should have checked the road report."

"I think we should get us a coffee maker," she said. "It'll save $25 a month."

"A coffee maker?" He shrugged. "OK."

Whitney leaned down to slide the transfer gearshift into high four-wheel and his hand brushed her leg. She scooted closer, nudged him with her knee.

"Careful not to knock it out of gear," he said.

The chains clinked with the first slow revolution, gripping the blacktop beneath the snow. Emma Lee put her head back and told herself that Whitney was a good man, even if he loved another woman. She'd only seen her once, on a night when they stopped for pie at the North Fork Diner on their way home from a doctor's appointment in Missoula. Her name tag said Ruby, and Emma Lee recognized the look she gave Whitney, so much the same as her own. Whitney tipped her too much, pretending not to notice when Emma Lee mentioned it on the car ride home. Later, he stared out the kitchen window for twenty minutes with a glass of water in his hand until she told him to sit.

Whitney turned down the heater. The truck smelled like him, like home: wood smoke, cooked hamburger, pinesap, aftershave, the musky scent of animal hides. They drove two miles before stopping to check the chains again, then onward. It was almost six o'clock, and the evening was made darker by the dense Ponderosa byway, brightened by the snow flitting in the headlights.

Emma Lee sat upright, hypnotized by the darting snow. Watching it was so much like the game of saying a word over and over until it lost its meaning. She craved that numbing sensation, was easily transfixed by the musicality of the snowflakes ticking, windshield wipers swishing, and she felt herself slip away to that otherworld. She thought of the Easter she and her mother and father and two older sisters folded themselves into the single cab of the ranch rig, each in their Sunday best. Emma Lee was five years old and she rode closest to the passenger door. A spring snow had settled over the hayfields and lowered the heads of sage buttercup on the hillside above the house. That morning her sisters had taught her how to puncture an egg with a needle to slowly release its insides, leaving the shell perfectly intact. She'd painted purple tulips on the egg, and it was the flowered egg she held in her hands when the truck door opened and she fell out.

Her father was driving and he stopped when her mother screamed. Emma Lee didn't remember the fall, only looking up to the flicker of taillights, to her father rounding the backend, not running but moving quickly, his face weathered with worry. She was still holding the egg, crushed between her hands, when he stood her up and brushed the snow from her dress.

Emma Lee looked at Whitney, his gaze so intent on the road, and she wished to fall out of the moving truck, to see the panic on his face, to feel the strength and warmth of his hands as he lifted her from the snowbank. She wanted him to feel the true weight of her absence, to show that he felt something, anything, toward her. When she left in September, she had every intention of staying gone, but then if life were governed by intentions, she wouldn't be pregnant in the first place. It was Whitney who said at the end of every phone call that he was sorry—he wasn't trying for any of this.

Emma Lee touched the cold door handle. If I wasn't pregnant, she thought, I'd do it. She touched her belly again, felt the pressure of the baby and pressure on her bladder. She squeezed her hand between her thighs. "I know you don't wanna hear this," she said, "but I've gotta pee."

Whitney took off his baseball cap and scratched his head. "There's another outhouse this side of Stanley Lake, if you think you can hold it."

"I'll try."

"It's a little ways, but you don't have much of a choice."

"I know that," she said. Now she did want to tell Whitney how much he sounded like her father, and how much she hated it.

"I can't go over forty with the chains."

"I'm not asking you to."

Whitney gripped the gearshift. "I need a dip," he said. "Hand me my spitter."

Emma Lee unfastened the seatbelt, bent forward and patted the floorboard. She felt the bottle slip past her hand and roll under the seat. "I can't find it," she said.

"Will you look again?"

"It hurts to bend like that. Let me turn on the light."

"No," he said. "I already can't see."

Emma Lee fastened the seatbelt. "The snow seems to be letting up some," she said. "I think we're driving out of it."

Whitney drove another five miles before pulling to the shoulder and removing the chains. When he finished, he walked to the passenger side and tried to open the door. It was locked and he knocked on the glass with his knuckle. Emma Lee rolled down the window.

"You wanna try now?" he said. "I can hold your arms while you squat."

"I don't want you to see me like that."

"I'm gonna see you in worse ways come March."

"You think so? You're staying above the shoulders." She pulled her hair into a ponytail. "My dad wasn't even in the room when I was born."

Whitney shook his head. It was no use trying to argue with her. He pinched a chew and tucked it into his bottom lip. The wind nearly stole his cap as he walked to the driver's side. The storm was behind them, or rather, they were ahead of it. In the headlights he could see the deep snow of the Sawtooth Valley, old snow that was peppered with deer and elk tracks.

Whitney accelerated and braked to check for black ice, but the road was mostly dry. Soon they were moving downhill in earnest, the descent about to give way to a series of rolling hills, then the long straightaway that led to the small town of Stanley. Every few miles the truck gave rise to a frost heave that made Emma Lee squeeze her thighs and moan. She was holding herself the way that small girls did before they knew better.

"You gonna make it?"

She moaned.

"Well?"

"I have to go too bad to talk."

He laughed. "Then stop talking."

"Then stop talking to me," she said. "And for God's sake, speed up."

Whitney sped up. "Dammit," he said. "I forgot to look for my spitter." He took one hand off the wheel and felt blindly across the floorboard.

Emma Lee watched him. She said, "You want me to steer?"

She looked back to the road and her eyes fell over the reflector of a mile marker, then the yellow eyes of a spike bull elk as it stepped out of the trees. She called Whitney's name, and because she could muster no other words, she closed her eyes and pointed.

At the sound of Emma Lee's voice, Whitney lifted his hand from the floorboard and stretched it over her. He hit the brakes and the truck hit the elk on the passenger side. A brown mass traveled up over the hood and smashed the windshield into a thousand-piece mosaic, the glass shattered but still intact.

He steered the truck to the side of the road. His ears were ringing. Emma Lee covered her face with her hands. He said her name too loudly, and she said, "My God, Whit, I'm right here."

The rumpled hood looked as delicate as paper. One headlight shone into the forest. Whitney put his hands on his head, then beat his fist once against the steering wheel. "Shit," he said. "Are you all right?"

He turned on the dome light. A dark spot on the hem of Emma Lee's sweatshirt spread over her pants and onto the seat. "Oh God," he said. "You're wet." He looked at her face. "Oh God, the baby—what does that mean?"

She didn't answer. He took hold of her arm and she shouldered away. "It means I wet myself, Whit. That's what it means. Please don't go getting all worked up about it. I'm already embarrassed." She crossed her arms. "I told you I had to go."

Whitney laughed, an honest and hardy laugh, and Emma Lee tried to laugh with him. He cut the engine and clicked the hazards for the second time that day. He opened the door and leaned out to spit.

"You smell that?" he said.

"Oh shut up already."

"Not you," he said.

The sweet maple smell of antifreeze filled the truck. Emma Lee's face fell slack. "The radiator," he said. "We're not going anywhere tonight."

Emma Lee turned from side to side. The truck cab felt like a coffin. She thought about avalanche victims and how they were supposed to swim to create air pockets in the snow. She wondered how anybody could remember such a thing when the world came falling down. The most she'd thought when they hit the elk was if Whitney had paid the truck insurance.

They sat quiet, the engine ticking. A faint cry lit the night, followed by a series of shorter, low-pitched moans that carried like an echo. Emma Lee looked at Whitney. He knew that sound. He'd heard variations of it before, from bullet-wounded deer or elk. He guessed the elk's back was broken and it was trying to get up. He couldn't be sure where it had landed—forty, maybe fifty yards behind them, and on the other side of the snow berm. The elk cried again, and it was unnerving how much it sounded like a human.

Emma Lee clasped both hands over her mouth. "Whit," she said, "you have to do something."

"I can't."

"You've got your pistol, don't you?"

"The state of Idaho says you can't harvest road kill. If I finish off that elk, you better believe the Fish and Game warden will be up here digging out the bullet. They'll take away my hunting license, and you know we can't afford that."

"But we're not harvesting. We're putting it out of its misery."

"It's the law," Whitney said. He turned on the stereo. They were a hundred miles from a radio station and he turned up the static to drown the elk's cries. He raised his voice when he said, "It'll die soon enough. Try not to think about it."

Emma Lee turned off the radio. "Aren't you gonna get out and look?"

"I'm not sure I want to."

"What about the truck? When was the last time you passed another car?"

He thought about it. He considered lying but didn't. "Garden Valley."

"That long ago?"

"Don't worry. Someone will come along. Someone always does."

"But what if they closed the pass? What if they lowered the avalanche gates?"

"I don't know." Whitney shook his head. "No, they can't do that. They have to send someone over to make sure there ain't nobody left traveling."

"Unless there was an avalanche and they can't get nobody over."

"I doubt it," he said. He thought it was too early in the season for an avalanche. And yet, he knew as well as anybody that the only certainty in this part of the country was the weather's ability to defy logic.

"Just think about it," she said. "An avalanche behind us, the highway closed in front of us, and here we are stuck in the middle."

He looked at her and tried to smile. "I reckon we ought to get comfortable."

Emma Lee put her hands back in the sweatshirt pocket. He wanted to tell her everything was going to be all right, but he didn't believe it.

"You want me to get you some dry clothes?" he offered.

"Yeah, OK," she said. "Whatever you can find."

Whitney came back with a can of peaches, a sleeping bag, a flashlight, emergency heat candles, sweatpants, Emma Lee's winter coat, and a pair of baby bloomers. He put it all on the seat between them.

"Truck looks bad," he said. "Looks expensive."

"Did you see the elk? I can't hear it anymore."

"No," he said. "It's dead now, I'm sure."

Emma Lee held up the can of peaches. "Why'd you bring these?"

"Thought you might be hungry." He paused. "You're hungry, aren't you?"

"Yes," she said. She held up the ruffled bloomers. "And this?"

Whitney turned it over in his hands and frowned. He held it to the light. "Hell," he said, "I thought it was your underwear."

Emma Lee laughed. "You've got a lot to learn about women, don't you? I don't know how you got me pregnant in the first place."

"It was an accident," he said.

She looked at him, his face sallow in the dome light. The windows were beginning to fog. She was cold and wet and uncomfortable. "You know I don't like the sound of that. I don't know why you keep saying it."

"I'm sorry," he said. "There ain't no other way to say it."

Emma Lee took off her sweatshirt and he saw for the first time the little mound of her belly. She'd always been thin and he hadn't been able to imagine her any other way. He looked at her breasts, at the way they pushed against her bra, at the folds of skin around her armpits, and he felt as if he'd never seen her before, as if they were two strangers sharing a ride to the same place.

She undressed from the waist down, and Whitney turned and looked out the window, at his reflection against the night.

"There," she said. She stepped into the sleeping bag and zipped it up. "Whit," she said, "someone's coming soon, right?"

Whitney didn't answer. He was thinking about the elk hunt again, about what had happened in the Bighorn Crags. They were following the tracks of a bull through the snow when Whitney heard a woman's voice call out from over the ridge—a distinct and clear voice riddled with fear. He stopped and lowered his ear. He said, "You hear that?" but the hunter shook his head and walked on. Whitney waited and listened, and in those passing seconds he couldn't be sure of anything except his greater instinct. He imagined a woman lost and wandering—someone's wife or mother, someone's Emma Lee—and it was enough to propel him forward. He turned to follow the voice, leaving the hunter alone in the steep terrain of the Frank Church Wilderness. It was a decision that had cost the hunter his elk, and it had cost Whitney his job.

Emma Lee said Whitney's name again, then a third time. Finally she leaned over and touched his shoulder and he jumped.

"Shit," he said. "Don't scare me like that."

She pulled away. "Who'd you think it was?"

He furrowed his brows. "I don't know."

Emma Lee felt a draft on all sides. She said in a whisper, "Where'd you go?"

"What?" he said. He turned off the dome light and they sat in the dark.

"Just then," she said. "You were somewhere else. You do that sometimes."

"So?"

"So it's like I don't exist. Here I am thinking, ok, he's concentrating hard, that's all. But then sometimes I look at you and it's like you don't exist. Like I don't know who you are anymore."

"For God's sake, Emma. You make it sound like I'm not doing everything right now for you and the baby." He turned to the window. "I haven't had a day off in three months. You think I like what I do for a living?" He forced a laugh, a laugh she had never heard. He held up his hands and turned them over. "I can't remember the last time I came home without my hands covered in grease or gas or pine sap or blood."

Emma Lee pulled the sleeping bag to her chin. "Tell me something, Whit. Tell me something no one else knows."

Whitney put his hands on his head. "I don't know a goddamned thing. I don't know up from down right now."

"Something," she said. "Just tell me something true."

Whitney sighed. "The truth is that sometimes there ain't nothing nice to talk about, Emma. There ain't nothing I can say that you wanna hear."

She squeezed his arm. "Anything."

"Emma, I don't know nothing about being pregnant, but I know this is your hormones talking."

"This is me," she said. "This is us talking and I need to hear you say it."

"What do you want me to say?"

"That this was an accident."

"I already said it."

"Say it again. Say it the way you mean it."

"That's not fair. I didn't ask for this."

"Say it," she said, her voice gathering tears.

"Fine. You're right. I don't want to be a father. Is that what you wanna hear? I don't know how to be a father. I can barely take care of myself. I can't even get us home safe."

Emma Lee was crying now. "But if it was somebody else," she said. "If it was somebody else, you might change your mind."

"Probably not," he said. "I don't know." He shook his head. "Hell, I don't know why we're even talking about this."

"But if it was her," she said.

"There ain't nobody else, Emma." He cut the air with his hand. "Look around. It's just us. There ain't nobody else around."

Emma Lee's shoulders shook the seat as she cried. It was cold enough to see her breath. Whitney tried to look out the shattered front windshield, then the side window, but the feathering of fern frost had begun to layer. No matter where he turned, Emma Lee's body slivered into his periphery.

He said, "Are you OK?" But she only drew in a breath.

"You should eat something." He took out his pocketknife and opened the can of peaches by the dim light of the dash. He offered the can to Emma Lee, but she shook her head. "Something," he said, "for the baby."

He positioned the can on the seat between them. In the truck's toolbox there was a six-pack of Gatorade, another two cans of peaches, and a Forest Service MRE of spaghetti and meatballs. By Whitney's estimate they were fourteen miles from Stanley. He knew of at least one roadside cabin along the way, and he thought if it was warm enough to snow, it was warm enough to walk. He knew better than to leave Emma Lee alone, but he couldn't sit there any longer.

"I'll be back," he said, and Emma Lee didn't protest. He opened the door and stepped into the night. He'd outrun the storm and now it was catching up with him. He could taste the snow coming—the taste of a cut lip, a taste like blood. The sky loomed heavy and close and he could only guess at the horizon's seam. From the truck's toolbox he retrieved a Gatorade, his down coat, and his hunting pack, still loaded from the week before. He glassed the backend with the flashlight, and it was then that he realized the car seat was gone.

Whitney walked in the middle of the road and his boots left no tracks in the patchwork snow. He worried a gloved hand against his coat hem as he considered, of all things, how to tell Emma Lee he'd lost his job. There was no simple answer. He'd abandoned the hunter to search out a voice only he had heard, and he'd come back empty-handed. He would tell Emma Lee the story, and he knew she would believe him, but that didn't seem to matter now. He listened to the wind whistle through the pine boughs, and he tried to remember the woman's voice, its urgency and pitch, but it was buried in a place he couldn't reach, like the residue of a dream.

Whitney had walked over a mile when he saw the flashing orange lights of the snowplow like a heartbeat in the dark. He waved and the snowplow flashed its headlights. He walked to the passenger side, and the driver leaned over and pushed the door open. Whitney climbed in.

"Thanks," he said.

The driver looked him over. "You got trouble?"

"I hit an elk about a mile up."

The driver shook his head. "Too bad. Just you driving?"

"No," Whitney said. He tried to think of what to call Emma Lee, but nothing felt right. "I'm with my—" he started, and the driver said, "Wife?"

Whitney nodded. He heard the faint singing of a woman on the stereo. The driver muted the volume, and Whitney listened to the engine lug through the low gears. The rear view mirror wore a necklace of Little Tree air fresheners, and the cab smelled of cigarette smoke and pine needles.

The driver looked to be the same age as Whitney, but he wore the mustache of an older man. He cleared his throat. "You from around here?"

"North Fork," Whitney said. "How about you?"

"Challis," the driver said, and they exchanged nods.

They stopped alongside the broken-down truck. It looked worse in the headlights than Whitney remembered.

"Damn," the driver said. "Must have been a big sucker."

The snow was coming down again, huge flakes that fluttered like a swarm of mayflies beating the black from their wings. Whitney thought by morning the truck would be no more than a rise in the landscape.

He tried to imagine what Emma Lee was doing right now, if she was angry with him. He wondered if she was still inside or if she had left him for good this time. He rubbed the back of his neck. No, of course she hadn't left. She had nowhere else to go.

The driver cracked his knuckles. He said, "I'll wait."

Emma Lee was asleep on the bench seat. Whitney opened the door and pulled the keys from the ignition. The empty can of peaches was turned over on the floorboard. Emma Lee sat up and blinked. The snowplow's headlights cast a muted glow through the iced-over windows. She had been dreaming, and now the dream escaped her, and she was cold again, colder. Whitney touched her shoulder, and it hurt to see him standing there, his face tired and empty, the red veins of his eyes like so many dead ends.

He motioned toward the snowplow. "Come on," he said. "Decide what you wanna take. There ain't room in there for much more than you and me."

Emma Lee put her hand to the frozen window. She said, "I don't want anything else."

BRUCE BOND
Chimera

The better the book, the more of us it reads.
Even as I look away, words float
across a world I never knew was there.

Page after page, I feel the light wind
breathe a little sense into things.
Why would it be any different with you.

I knew a man once who had one blue iris,
another green. Sisters, he called them,
born into the womb through separate lives,

each a sacrament eaten by the other.
When he talked, I wondered which of his
to answer, though that was my own eye talking.

There are those who believe we learn nothing
outside of what we know, as if wisdom
were a shovel, a hole. I have buried too much

to go there, to see time as motionless
as numbers, or claim, as numbers do, all things
die into memory where they await us.

Was it the me or I who led to this.
I want to say neither. My father taught me
to behave, and I loved that about him.

Sometimes he was cross at the table,
and we crumpled into tears. If he talked
when we were talking, our voices vanished.

A lot of books feel that way, I know.
The day he died, it set certain limits
the way a father does. If I say I visit

his body still, blame it on the twin stars.
Disbelief has eyes of different colors.
So dark, this ink, this emptiness between.

CATHERINE CARTER

Arson in Ladytown

> *"I hate Ladytown—so much can go wrong down there."*
> —*Steph*

Things weren't looking good in Ladytown.
True, it was always lush, like D.C. in August,
high humidity, but that year the very
brickwork sweated salt. That year
the Metro chafed the tunnel walls and the train
whistles' wail rose to a new pitch
of dismay, for that year there was to be
a procedure, proceeding God knew where.
And if you thought you had troubles before—
those eerie white fungi, the earthquakes
that wrung blood from the stones of the streets—
well. Now the arched gates were pried open
with steel rams. Now came the burning,
like misogynistic madmen were firing
the curtains and laying down flammables
in the bookstores and gardens and coffee shops
of Ladytown, shuddering the muscular
silky foundations Eggs scrambled themselves
on the shimmering asphalt. Ambulances
screamed in, firefighters didn't dare
sleep, flames licked and leapt from bramble
to billboard to hospital to house, men
fled clutching babies and books and balls.
It's easy to get tired of a city that someone
is burning around you. Easy to wish the town
would just get up and move out of the way,

no matter how it happened. Even the women
wished they lived somewhere else,
though there was nowhere for them to go,
all that blistering summer in Ladytown.

HARRY CLIFTON

Estación Retiro, Buenos Aires

A run-down hall of echoes. Shout your name,
You will hear it again, from generations
Gone before you . . . The souls they have become
By the million, look at them, transmigrating

Out of Europe, dragging sailors' trunks
Aboard the Pullmans—conscious of rank,
Edwardian . . . There they go, to break the bank
Of the Gran Chaco, fornicate, die drunk

In an age of uprootings. One who flipped a coin
For South America, one evading War,
One who blew himself up, on the lonely floor
Of his own outstation. Dead, reborn

In the place of eternal return, is it any wonder
You hesitate, in thirty centigrade air,
A wilderness of shimmering track out there
Beyond the platforms, so many dead behind you,

Fathers and forefathers? Not to pass
Or live them through again at ticket-control,
The million immigrant lives that shoot like grass
Between the tracks—is praxis of the soul.

TESSA HADLEY
Post Production

Albert Arno, the film director, dropped dead at his home in the middle of a sentence. It was early evening and his wife, Lynne, was lifting a dish of potato gratin out of the oven. Albert came out of the downstairs shower room, one striped towel wrapped round his waist, rubbing his neck with another: a fit man in his mid-sixties, not tall, with a thick white torso and a shock of silvering hair.

"Oh good," he said, seeing her lift out the dish in padded oven gloves. "I'm hungry, I…"

Then he dropped to the floor as dramatically as if he'd been felled by a blow from behind. While she dashed down the gratin dish on the kitchen surface, Lynne thought that was what must have happened, though she couldn't see what had hit him; he hadn't shouted, or given out any noise except an abrupt exhalation of surprise, as if the breath was knocked out of him. When his weight hit the floor, the noise was awful. A wooden stool went flying with a clatter. Lynne ran over thinking she was going to help him up; when she touched his chest, she knew that it was empty.

Albert was still warm, he was still unmistakably himself, as he had been in the fullness of his energetic toweling a few seconds ago. Lynne couldn't take in that it wasn't possible to reenter those seconds and pull things back into their real, familiar order. He had fallen awkwardly, on his back but twisted to one side, legs splayed; the towel round his waist had untwisted, and she pulled it across to cover his suddenly vulnerable penis, exposed limp in its nest of hair. She couldn't possibly lift him, yet she could feel the cold coming up through these old slates, laid directly on the earth. Even as she snatched at the phone to dial 999, she was running through to the boiler room behind the kitchen. She could use the old picnic blankets, kept folded on a shelf. The boiler was ticking over comfortably, privately, as if everything were going on as usual.

Albert's eyes were open. That was the worst thing, Lynne thought. There was some shame involved in his blind stare: he was caught out, or she was caught out, seeing him see nothing. Trying to tuck the blankets in around him, she wasn't aware that she was making some kind of hiccuping noise, low-level crying, until she tried to talk at the same time to the emergency services. Then she consciously calmed herself down. She must take charge. They told her the ambulance would be with her within twenty to thirty minutes. The house was at the back of beyond, in rural Dorset.

"I'm going to call my husband's brother," she said. "He knows first aid."

At the idea of calling Ben, Albert's producer and business partner, the squeezing around Lynne's heart eased somewhat. Ben almost lived with them, they saw him every day; Lynne imagined the phone breaking in on the peace of his little cottage, a ten-minute walk away. Now he would be turning down the classical music he was listening to, or putting down his book. She felt dread and regret at the news she had to pour out for him, curdling everything.

"I'm on my way," he said. "Hold on."

Lynne's son Tom, Albert's stepson, was asleep in his room upstairs. She had thought Tom would come running when he heard the crash; but the fall—and her cry, she must have cried out—might not have woken him, the house had thick old walls. Tom had been sleeping a lot since he came home (he was depressed; he was threatening that he wouldn't go back to finish his degree at Oxford). Lynne couldn't worry about him, at this moment. It was using up all of her work, sitting beside her husband's body, holding on to his unresponsive hand.

"Ben's on his way," she reassured him.

Those minutes when she had the house all to herself were mysteriously rich. Whatever was coming had not broken yet, in the adrenalin rush of the moment, over her head. Would it be grief? What would that be like? She stood up once and crossed the kitchen to open the back door, to listen for Ben. Outside, the moon stood in a blurry ring of bronze light. Hail that had fallen earlier was scattered in its tiny perfect spheres on the grass and the paths and the roofs of the outhouses, which were workshops and studios, making them luminous. The sculptures—a stone nymph and garlanded boy, a warrior made from scrap metal—seemed alive, caught mid-movement. It was so quiet. Albert had a big voice; if he was talking on the telephone, you couldn't carry on your own conversation, you weren't meant to. Even in his taciturn moods he was always on the move, banging doors, running the bath or the shower, playing loud music or the radio.

Ben arrived in the Lamborghini, tires crunched on the frozen gravel, the luxuriating engine cut. Then he was with her in the kitchen, kneeling beside Albert, feeling for a pulse. Ben didn't look anything like his brother. Albert's hair was jet black when she first knew him, his beard grew strongly, his mouth was red and wet; Ben had pale hair, a long mournful intelligent face. Albert looked like their Jewish mother.

"He's gone, sweetheart," Ben said, and he reached over and closed Albert's eyes.

"Isn't there anything we ought to try?"

"No. Leave him in his peace."

Tears were rolling down Ben's cheeks, although he was quite calm. Lynne was surprised at herself that she wasn't crying. He clasped her against him; she felt waves of weeping shuddering through her brother-in-law's diaphragm. After a minute or two, however, when he put her gently away from him, he didn't look in the least ravaged or out of control. He arranged Albert's body so that he was lying on his back, covered neatly with the blankets. Then he turned off the oven and began cleaning up the mess, with bowls of soapy water: where Lynne had slammed down the potato gratin on the ceramic-tiled kitchen surface, she had cracked the dish, and the creamy fatty juices were trickling down the front of the cupboards and into a pool on the floor. She hadn't even noticed this, all the time she was sitting there alone with Albert.

"You go with him," Ben said when the ambulance came. "I'll take care of Tom. I'll tell him what's happened. I'll drive to the hospital as soon as I've done that. I'll come and get you."

Lynne assumed that without Albert, the whole film enterprise that had been their lives would grind to a halt forever. Albert had been the genius, the rest of them had simply gone along with him. When she met and married him, eighteen years ago (Tom was just two years old), the machinery of Albert's importance and career had already been in place; she'd never known him when he wasn't a famous man. She had worked on films before she met him but only in a production office, she wasn't creative. In the days following the funeral, Lynne recovered all the old worshipping love she'd felt for Albert when they were first together. Sleep was the worst because she had to wake up to the loss all over again.

She began to understand that the *Elective Affinities* could not be abandoned. The completion guarantee would fund them to bring in another director—only Ros apparently wanted to finish it without outside help. Ros was Albert's indispensable editor, his partner in vision (he had called her that). Diminutive and fiery, she had come to the funeral in dark glasses, face ugly from weeping, her long mass of dyed bright auburn curls tied back in a black scarf. Ben said she had all Albert's notes, she'd been at his side every moment of filming.

Lynne doubted. "How can we know for sure what was in Albert's mind?"

Ben made her understand that they had to go ahead, in any case, whoever took over. Anyway, how could they not finish it? The film was in the can, it was going to be something beautiful.

Later she stood in front of the full-length mirror, in the bedroom she had shared with Albert, wearing her long silk écru nightdress, trimmed in chocolate lace—now he was gone, she saw she was too old for it, in her fifties. Her skin was chalky, her cheekbones jutted, her hair was dry as straw. When she heard Ben's key turn in the front door, she called to him to come upstairs. He had been in and out of the house all day, there was always business to transact from the office. Lynne felt self-conscious in her nightdress; Ben was in his camel overcoat, his long cheeks pink from his walk up from the cottage. The bedroom must seem stiflingly hot to anyone coming in from outside. He said he was worried he'd been overbearing when he quashed her doubts about going ahead with the film. "It's your call, you ought to have the last word. It doesn't matter what Ros thinks. Maybe you'd rather we brought in another director? Take time to think about it."

She didn't need time. They must have Ros, to do justice to the film.

She knew Ben, how, under his controlled surface, his conscience labored subtly and was always in turmoil. Now that Albert was dead, she would become part of what he had to worry over.

Tom flung himself full length on the bed, face down, voice muffled in the pillows.

"What's Ben sniffing round after?"

Lynne was taking off her makeup at the dressing table. "Ben's so loyal, looking out for us."

"There's nothing old Uncle Ben can do for me."

As Albert would have pointed out if he'd been there, Tom was behaving as usual, as if the whole disaster had only happened to him. Albert had sometimes held his stepson off with cold disdain, at other times reeled him in, talking to him late into the night: especially once it was clear that Tom was clever. He was good-looking too, with raw unfinished cheekbones, small blue-black eyes set in deep sockets. With his white skin and dark hair he could easily have been taken for Albert's son, although he was languid and tall, instead of blocky and stolid.

"Ben's just a businessman," Tom said. "If it wasn't for Dad, he'd be a used-car salesman."

"You're a ghastly snob."

"And he's homophobic."

"Rubbish."

Lynne explained Ben's scruple, over Ros' taking over the direction of the *Affinities;* Tom couldn't object to that, he had always adored Ros, he had toddled round after her when he was a finicky baby with a cuddle blanket.

"You're not thinking about what Dad's death means for me," he said, "my future as an actor."

"I didn't even know you wanted to be an actor."

"All the doors he could have opened for me. I'm finished now."

Lynne put her hand on Tom's high white forehead. "It's not you that's finished, sweetheart. You're not finished yet."

"And I'm not convinced Ben is so family minded. Unless you're talking really Old Testament. Uncle Ben's on your scent, Ma. He's after you."

"Go to bed, Tom, please, if you can't be sensible. I want to be by myself."

He burst into loud tears. "I know I'm behaving like a cunt. I just can't bear it that he's gone."

She put her arms around him, lying down on the bed beside him. "I can't bear it, either, darling. But we have to."

He went eventually, reluctantly, carrying away one of her pillows.

Tom used to try all sorts of tricks, when he was a little boy, to get to stay in Lynne's bed at night and fall asleep with her. When Albert came in later (he always came to bed very late), he would carry the sleeping boy in his pajamas back to his own room. For a moment this ritual, so tender and intent, was vividly real to Lynne, more substantial and lasting than anything in the present: as if she could hear Albert's step, careful with his burden, on the landing.

The post-production team worked to be faithful to every last detail of what Albert had imagined for *Elective Affinities*. Excitement buoyed them up eerily and sadly. Lynne was glad that all of this unfolded around her in her home. Jacquie visited, his queenly agent, terribly upset and kind. The Italian distributors tried to pull out. Ros' personality emerged with a new definiteness, without Albert: forthright, reckless in her personal relations, with a scalding flaring humor. She quarreled with the indispensable Leo, Ben's assistant. With Lynne she was guarded, they didn't talk much, though scrupulously she invited Lynne to look at the cut sequences as they came together. Lynne said she'd rather wait and see the whole thing. Two little furrows of misery had settled in the golden skin of Ros' face, beside the brightly red-lipsticked mouth; she often wore her dark glasses, which looked affected in the middle of winter. In February she turned forty. "Don't dare say one word, anyone!" she warned one Monday morning, unwinding her scarf from round her head in the kitchen, shaking heavy silver earrings. She had had all her mass of orange curls shorn off over the weekend. Free of its headdress of hair, the queer long handsome face was bleakly naked, spectacular. Tom, who was wearing Albert's old pajamas while making his breakfast coffee at the stove (his tutor at Oxford had advised him to take a year out), bent ceremoniously and kissed the gingery stubble.

Lynne and Ben often ate alone together, if the team went down to the pub for supper and Tom went with them. Sometimes Ben cooked for her in the cottage. Their relations were easy, grieving together. When Lynne went up to London to see the lawyers, Ben took her out to dinner. Lynne pretended to take no notice of the things Tom said about Ben: but the truth was, his insinuations slipped under her skin, shaming her, changing her awareness of how her brother-in-law helped her into her coat, rested his arm across her shoulders, was unfailingly considerate of her feelings and well-being. He was her dear old friend, nothing of the sort had ever come up between them in the past; he might be appalled if he knew what Tom had planted in her thoughts. Nonetheless, Lynne was ambushed by excitements she had thought written off forever when her hormones changed.

"He's after your money, Ma," Tom said. "He wants total control of the business."

He surely didn't believe any of this.

"You've loved being the wife of an important artist. The kudos, the creativity, the parties. Don't make a mistake and settle for a mediocrity."

Surprising herself, Lynne slapped her son hard, leaving a pink mark on his cheek.

Leo organized a screening of Ros' cut in their little cinema: an intimate occasion, for the post-production team and a few friends—Jacquie came down, John Hay who was writing the music, Deborah Jones who played Ottilie and had been close to Albert. Tom was sweetly sympathetic when he found Lynne turning out her wardrobe in tears, convinced she had nothing to wear; they chose black crepe trousers and a green silk Nicole Farhi jacket.

The film began with the married couple in a garden. It was Lynne who first suggested that Albert should take a look at this novel, which she had studied at university. His screenplay wasn't anything like the story she remembered: to begin with, he had translated it into the present day. But in any case, she could hardly concentrate on what was supposed to be happening between the four characters—all she was conscious of was Albert, present in every shot as if he'd returned from the dead. She could only see back into the camera's eye, and into what lay behind the eye. At one point of heightened emotion between the film lovers, Lynne was so painfully carried outside herself that she twisted round in her seat, as if she might try getting out over the back of it. It had been a mistake to accept a seat in the front row, where she couldn't escape without disrupting everyone. Ben restrained her and put his hand on her knee to comfort her. In the few months since Albert died, Lynne thought, she had already begun smoothing him out, making a doll of him. His cold will used to grate against her often, sometimes he had bored her; it was a relief to be delivered out of his orbit. But now everything was lost: all the scattered effect of a real person, complicated beyond counting.

After the screening, they gathered in the house for a party, which was a kind of wake. Everyone got drunk very quickly. It was still cool enough in May for a wood fire in the cavernous stone hearth; when they drank to Albert, they threw their glasses to smash in the back of the fireplace. Jacquie wept, and Deborah—who was sensible and funny, beautiful in jeans and baggy jumper. People made speeches about Albert's rare vision of people, tender and penetrating. Lynne circulated round her old friends, she thrust the memory of the film behind her. Everyone said it was a masterpiece. Lynne thought Ros looked strained and ill, but that might have just been her different hair.

When Lynne said goodnight, hours later, the young ones were dancing somewhere in a back room. Climbing the stairs, she had to hang on to the banister rail, she was so tired. When she opened the door of her bedroom, she wasn't sure straight away what it was she was seeing, or who it was, on top of her duvet: she had never seen sex before, in real life, from this angle, from outside: legs splayed, feet waving in the air, buttocks pumping in a motion that made her think of insects. It was as if someone was taken ill. Her heart lunged: the exposure was hers, from having witnessed this. She shut the door hastily, hoping they hadn't heard her, and sat down to think about it on the stairs. Then again, she hoped they had heard her. She had drunk quite a lot.

Of course: Albert had been fucking Ros. No wonder Ros was brokenhearted.

But it didn't really matter.

Ben came out into the hall below, not seeing her, folding his scarf neatly round his neck for the walk home. She leaned over the banister, drawing his attention in an exaggerated whisper.

"I can't go in the bedroom," she said, making a game of it.

"What?"

Taking off her shoes, she tiptoed down with her finger to her lips. The party was still audible at the other end of the house. She held the lapels of his camel-hair coat, to explain in his ear that Tom and Ros were in her bedroom. Making love, she said.

"You've got to be kidding. Anyway, I thought that Tom liked boys?"

"Well, he does. Though he was going at it fairly energetically. I suppose he's got this thing about his Dad. About Albert. I expect that's why they're doing it on my bed. Because they both had a thing about Albert."

"D'you want me to go and bawl them out about it?"

"Certainly not. How awful would that be? I only don't know where to lay my head, tonight. Do you think I could come and stay at the cottage?"

Ben was holding on to her, puzzling into her face. He wasn't good-looking, not the kind of man she'd ever have gone for when she was younger and could have her pick. But now she felt the glamour in his steady courtesy and calm, his competence.

"As long as you know," Ben said.

"Know what?"

"That it'll be hard for me. Having you at such close quarters and not taking advantage."

She laid her cheek against the expensive softness of his coat.

The four of them gathered together on the anniversary of Albert's death, at the bottom of the slump between Christmas and New Year: Lynne and Ben, Tom and Ros. Ros was in her last trimester of her pregnancy, which sat high on her tiny frame like a football. Ben had moved up into the house, Tom and Ros had taken over the cottage. There must have been some delicious gossip. Ros had mostly been away, working on a new project for a director in the u.s., then promoting the *Affinities;* now she had scheduled herself a break for a few months. She was working on a screenplay, hoping to direct a feature of her own.

Ros wanted to go for a walk, but Tom was too lazy, sprawled smoking beside the fire with his socks almost in the ashes, reading through all the sections of the paper. Although he was supposed to have moved down to the cottage, he still spent most of every day in the big house. Lynne came in her striped apron from the kitchen, where she was stuffing a joint of pork for later. Ben was sending e-mails in the office. Ros stood impatiently in her bright blue coat, its buttons strained across her bump. Her hair had grown, she was dyeing it orange again, she had it wrapped in a vermilion knitted scarf.

"You're such a slob. You ought to be disgusted with yourself."

"Aren't I a slob?" Tom commiserated complacently, waggling his toes.

Untying her apron, Lynne volunteered. "I'll go with you. I'd like a walk."

Ros had to appear to be grateful: but it was probably the last thing she wanted. The two women were so unlike, bound together in such convoluted circumstances; Lynne guessed that Ros found this unbearable sometimes, though their mutual politeness had never faltered. Lynne had never said a word, to accuse Ros. Beside Ros, she felt herself bleached of color, old and ordinary; yet she found herself making these clumsy efforts to get closer to the younger woman. They drove to the Iron Age fort a few miles down the road; an unkempt oval mound rearing austerely out of the farmed landscape. It was a few degrees colder up there than at the house—every leaf and blade of grass was outlined in frost crystals, and frozen mud crackled under their walking boots, though the sun was on their backs.

Ros waddled in her top-heavy roll along the path around the fort's perimeter, hands in her pockets, telling bright, funny stories about her experiences in the u.s. Although she was laughing, there was something dogged and bitter in how she threw herself along faster than she needed to, shoulders hunched defensively. They avoided the subject of *Elective Affinities,* which opened in a few weeks. Where the path narrowed and they had to walk in single file, Ros stopped short suddenly in pain, crouching over. She reassured Lynne breathlessly that these were only Braxton Hicks contractions, she was having them most days, her doctor said they were nothing to worry about, he didn't know why they were so painful.

"What a mess, this whole thing."

Lynne embraced her, awkwardly through the thickness of their winter wrappings, trying to rub where it hurt: Ros grabbed her hand and pushed it into the right place, under the blue coat. The rubbing seemed to help. It was the first time Lynne had touched this pregnancy—these days everyone wanted to put their hands on someone's bump, for luck, or marveling. In other periods, it had been a thing to keep hidden. Something seemed to convulse in the hard, hot mound under her hand.

"I didn't think I'd ever have a grandchild," Lynne said. "So I'm happy."

Ros looked wanly. "I'm glad someone's happy. I suppose I'll get used to it. But you do know Tom and I aren't a real couple? He doesn't really want to sleep with girls. This is only temporary. It was a kind of accident.

Lynne said of course she knew, it didn't matter.

Walking on, Ros spilled over with her fears, deferring to Lynne as an expert. They were still in single file; Lynne, coming behind, had to strain to catch everything she said. She had never heard Ros sound like this before: unsure of herself, and even querulous. She said she was dreading that she would be a bad mother; Lynne reassured her she would muddle along like everyone did. Wasn't it irresponsible to conceive a child outside a stable relationship? Lynne told her about Tom's father, who used to hit her and then blame her for provoking him. The last sloes were withered on the blackthorn bushes. Usually Lynne came to the fort to pick them in the autumn. She and Albert had picked sloes here in the October before he died; they had meant to drink the sloe gin on her birthday in February, but when that time came, she naturally hadn't given it a thought. It must be waiting still, in its Kilner jar on the shelf in the boiler room. When she got home, she would look to see if it wasn't spoiled.

"Isn't it strange?" Ros said in a tearful excitable voice. "How we're all four still held together here? As if we can't escape from the pattern Albert made out of our lives, connecting us, even now he's gone."

Lynne said blandly that she didn't think about it like that.

She didn't care if people imagined she was only with Ben for convenience; she liked to shield their relationship from prying eyes. When she took him his coffee in the office, she pulled the door shut behind her so that they could be alone together for five minutes; then she might only sit holding his hand. As a lover, he was decorous and shy. They were only beginning to get to know each other.

Lynne cried off from attending the premiere of *Elective Affinities*, though Ben tried to persuade her to go. There were wonderful reviews. Weeks afterward, when she was staying with her sister in Faversham, she went to see the film by herself one afternoon, telling her sister she was going shopping, paying for a ticket, and slipping into the back of a cinema, where there were only five or six other people, most of them solitaries like her. She could hardly connect what she saw now to her experience of the film at the private screening. Every scene then had seemed charged with terrible revelation; she must have been slightly mad, at that point in her mourning. Because the film was really only a comedy, a love story, or a grown-up succession of love stories, tracing the intricate shifts of affection and desire around a set of close friends. Lynne didn't weep once as she watched, she was very calm; although she also felt herself laid open to the film, the scenes washing through and through her, with their beautiful imagery: winter trees, light and dark reflections on water, Deborah's character's green dress flitting past the windows of a house, her aunt's lover watching surreptitiously from inside.

Lynne gave herself up to the dream Albert had brought into being, hardly conscious this time of his controlling presence. When it was finished, she caught a bus back to where her sister lived, outside the town. It was the end of a wet afternoon; the waterproofs of shoppers were slick with wet, they were tired, laden with carrier bags. Lynne felt the power of the film pooled inside her, glimmering and gray, something to live by. Meanwhile, she gave herself over to the ordinary dirty traffic, the laboring stop-start of her bus journey, the smells of wet wool and hair and trainers, and the motley collection of passengers, mostly not talking to one another, only into their mobiles.

MICHAEL DICKMAN
Home

In Heaven
ants are the doormen
to the flies

I climbed out of one butchered ballroom into another climbing out
      of my half-life into my new life on earth

My brother right behind me

Home

The ants are a straight line of suicides
showing us the way
out of here

The flies are suicides
with wings

They live in shit

We lived in a little blue house with a maple tree in the front yard

One ballroom and then

another

*

I've always wanted my body
to work harder
at being
alive

The light you see in veins

Eyelids eye-
lids

Snow

I stood in the yard and looked up at the wires in the leaves their
       eyelids turning red blinking on and off

My body won't do what I want it to
It won't burn

It says   I hold your hands in snow

In my hands

I hold your face

*

What you want to remember
of the earth
and what you end up
remembering

The flies get stuck between the single-pane and the storm windows
       turning up the volume on everything

I could stay here for such a long time

And not go anywhere
not even with you
not even if you were

finally leaving

But your voice
there in front of me
where I am going
to live

GERARD FANNING
Toss

Every year they come together
like the risen sap of bamboo,
cross cut canes pitch and toss,
all the families waving, in the white
laden branches of the pear trees.

Hives that once sang like choirs
lie against the gable walls
of their churches and schools,
tossed in the dust of quarantine,
old tea chests, apothecaries' desks.

They are praying, you see, with their
legs and arms coated in pollen,
that these fleeting caresses can give
hope to the smocks and dresses that live
as a ripening swell in the blossom.

GERARD FANNING
An Old Boyne Fish Barn

You should have seen the sea in those days,
wind smoke and weeping flares washing

ashore from the barrios, all those
hesitant evacuees, as tarpaulin stretched

along Beaufort's Dyke and our drift nets
sailed through the Hebrides. Shuffling in pipe

smoke, scribbling a plume of grave longing
on the bones of a wax-bright dusk,

I stood to see the ranks at the fish barn—
open mouthed, open boxed, iced on shelf

after shelf—and stayed to inhabit
what remains for the solipsistic raconteur

who believes the weight of his vision
will dissolve with his last sigh. When I drag

a heavy catch out of the evening,
old weather, braced for meteorites,

groans like a dehumidifier and burbles
the gospel of faith and love and water.

GERARD FANNING
Memoire

It seems farfetched, I know,
but when we tethered toy horses
in the lea of the patio

the moon wept like a candle,
and the dawn when it came
crept along the dusty panhandle.

Best not to worry the truth
like that yarn about Turner
strapped to the mast

of the little ice age,
better to understand
sea spray and corn wave

and the years without a summer,
better to remain indoors, secretive,
unreliable, like a memoire.

GERARD FANNING
Tall Boys

In Leeson Street
we find ourselves

in a Georgian chapel of ease,
an elite mass rock,

in an Irish lexicon,
in a credo unravelling,

in ambivalent government attire,
we stand, genuflect,

stand again and disperse,
miming handshakes

and the bluster of concern.
What stains our hands—

March as before
whipped in a narrow light—

as we peer into
Fitzwilliam's forbidden park,

are the old yarns snoozing
beneath the clipped grass

and all the dead tall boys
who made the winters fast.

GERARD FANNING
In My Reading

If there is such a thing anymore
as a humble servant in the vineyard

this is he, a man from the coast
home on his lunch break

working the stooped enclosure
below me as I read and revel

in the feral words of murder
on what passes for a roof garden

with a view of Pompeii
and further below

through French doors,
you sleeping, an afternoon to dream

or pray after the heat of love making,
just as his turning broken clay

with a method learned as a boy
becomes a kind of recreation

to justify and while away
olive baskets filled with autumn

as his mother, who once
combed her hair like Myrna Loy,

watches with approval
this noise of renewal

or so it appears
in my reading.

Natural Wonder

Once, when she'd been walking in her neighborhood, a car had stopped for directions to Alsop, the psychiatric hospital perched above the Blackstone River. How to get there was complicated, the man already so lost in the tangle of leafy streets that Tess hadn't been sure where to start. Begin at the beginning, wasn't that the trick? So she'd asked, "Do you know where you are?"

The man's smirk emerged from a fog of cigarette smoke. "Lady, if I knew where I was, would I be going to the nuthouse in the first place?"

They'd had a good laugh as the sun twitched behind the trees. She'd told the story to Eli that night, but later she wondered why she'd found it so funny. This was a few years before Ben did his own time at Alsop—and there was nothing particularly funny about her son droopy behind those metal doors. She was like that lost man now; did she have any idea where she even was? Her daughter had given her directions to the ski house up in the gullet of Vermont, precise distances, route numbers, and sharp turns, but they left her cold and without imagination. If Tess had been giving directions, she would have included the ice-encased apple orchard and the tennis courts like giant cribs blanketed in December's snow, sights to make you feel the long trip was worth it.

She was headed to Gorham, but where was she in relation to anything else? It wasn't like saying come to Paris, or Detroit, or the bedroom, or come to me, something she and Eli hadn't said to each other in a very long time. She'd meant to look at a map yesterday, but instead she'd gone out to buy a salami for Margot, a decision that now seemed ridiculous and striving. She could smell the thing stinking in the bag next to her. Take me, she would say to her daughter, take my sopressata, forgive my failings as your mother. And then she would add: your father and I are splitting up. Margot wouldn't take it so well.

She was certain she'd never been to this part of Vermont before, and yet here was a sign for Millboro, a town she'd spent a weekend in with Eli years ago. She was alarmed by how she'd gotten her geography wrong, as if it wasn't her memory that had drifted but the land itself. She took the exit out of curiosity, a need for gas, and no hurry to get to her daughter's, but nothing was familiar, not the gleaming Exxon station with its vivid declarations of snacks and sodas, not the stand of pines behind the idle school buses, not the way the land dipped away like the bowl of a ladle. But there was that July weekend she hadn't thought of in decades; fireflies, gin with curls of lime, two young couples so fat with the notion of endless time that she was embarrassed now by how little they knew. She considered calling Eli and saying, *guess what?* And, *guess where I am?* And, *guess how fast time goes?* But he would recall the weekend one way, she another, and where would that leave them but blinking into the familiar and sad silence between them?

Frigid air needled her skin as she pumped gas. There was a low roar, and a train of snowmobiles crested the snow and parked at the other set of pumps. The riders were fearsome in steroidily leather outfits. No, she wouldn't call Eli; that's not what they did anymore. The weekend had ended badly anyway, with the men fist fighting in the moonlight like insomniac pugilists. Memory did not preserve marriage like a child's tooth in a small white box. What she needed to consider now was everything ahead of her today—her formidable daughter, her son-in-law of a year, Kirk. Tess had told people she was looking forward to two nights at the ski house, Kirk's real estate booty from his first marriage, at the base of Wantusket Mountain, but really, how could she be. Margot could be like an ice pack you placed on your pain; flip her over and she might be even colder. And then there was the news Tess was bringing her. She glanced at the line of snowmobiles and left.

It was just after noon when she found the house, but already hints of evening were falling like ash. She didn't think her Mini, unlike the massive SUV at the top of the icy driveway, was going to make it, so she parked on the road and hauled out her bag. She hoped that someone would appear in one of the graceless A-frame's windows, but there were only reflections of the mountain it bowed before. Halfway up, she fell forward on her hands. Her knees smacked the ice and a sour taste rose from under her tongue. She wanted to rest her forehead on the ice for a moment, but she was a fifty-three-year-old in a green parka riding down on all fours; best to enjoy the slide. On her next try, she reached the house, knocked, and went inside, snow-blinded and rushed by humidity. It was like breathing in a swarm of gnats. In front of her was a steaming hot tub on a platform, and in the cauldron, like two overdone birds, were Margot and Kirk. Chlorine's stink banged through her sinuses.

"You made it," Margot said, her shoulders rising from the water. Kirk waved a beefy, dripping arm. "We thought you probably got lost."

"Nope. Perfect directions," Tess said. "Very exacting." Sweat was already collecting under her breasts and she took off her coat. "You didn't tell me there was a hot tub. I would have brought my suit."

"I did tell you," Margot corrected. "I guess you forgot."

At one point in the fully blossomed years of Margot's acidic adolescence, Tess had decided to swallow rather than spit out these small untruths and accusations from her daughter, restitution for having given her Ben as a brother. If someday they found a gristly knot in her gut, it would be made of acquiescence and guilt. Margot looked cooked, her short hair forming apostrophes on her forehead. At twenty-four, her features were already thick like Eli's peasant mother. She had none of Tess' thin tension. Kirk, fifteen years older, had the alien coloring of thinned-down carrot juice, and enthusiastically big nipples that bobbed on the water's surface like pool toys.

Tess asked him how the skiing had been that morning. Her question didn't require answering, but what could she do but nod at the fleshy son-in-law she barely knew? She assumed there was some fiddling going on under the water while Kirk talked avidly because Margot was starting to look disconnected.

"Hey buddy," Kirk said, removing his paw from the erotic depths.

Tess turned around to the palest child she'd ever seen. There was the suggestion of a bird's hollow skeleton beneath the bloodless skin and popcorn colored hair. He had red-rimmed, fetally lashless eyes, the faintest mouth like a cranberry juice stain.

"And who are you?" she asked. He was wearing a dirty white turtleneck and corduroy pants with a high elastic waist. All that was missing was a dunce cap.

"Ryan," Margot said.

"You didn't tell me—." Tess caught herself. She'd known the boy existed, of course, the ten-year-old output of Kirk's first marriage, but she definitely hadn't been told he'd be there.

"Say hello to your grandma, Ry," Kirk instructed. "Be polite, buddy."

Grandma—but she had nothing to do with this strange kid. She smiled at him. "Call me Tess, OK, sweetheart?" She talked to him like he was a rock, but there was something so absent about him it was like speaking to the box where you placed your drive-through order. You never knew if it went through.

"Hey, want to jump in, pal?" Kirk asked. "Take a soak, soldier?"

Buddy. Pal. Soldier. None of those idiotic, virile tags fit this wisp of a kid.

"But no peeing in the hot tub," Margot warned. "I mean it."

"I don't do that," he said, and mumbled *dumb-ass fucker lady* so Tess could hear.

"Do you ski too, Ryan?" she asked. She wished he wouldn't stand right behind her, like a stalker.

"I have a cold." He exhaled tepid, sour milk breath as evidence.

"But you're learning how, right, pal?" Kirk encouraged.

The boy gave his father a primal and blank look, and pivoted back to where he'd come from, a room abandoned except for a plaid chair and a television jammed in the corner. Margot stepped out of the tub, her black suit slick like mercury, and threw a towel across her shoulders. The fronts of her thighs were glistening slabs of ham. She led Tess to a wood-paneled bedroom in the back, the flow of green indoor-outdoor carpet uninterrupted. The house was wedged into the side of a hill, and the bedroom's lone window was black with snow that pressed against it.

Margot sat on one of the two single beds. "Just so you know, I didn't know Ryan was coming," she said. "A so-called last-minute emergency with his mother."

"It's fine. He's cute. It will be fun."

Margot's eyebrows lifted. "Cute? Not sure about that."

"Yes, cute. All kids are cute," Tess said. "In their own way."

What did her daughter, with her small and pinched sympathies, know about being a stepmother? What had she ever learned from Tess who strained at the seams with mistakes? Margot worked in the public affairs office of the American Heart Association, an incongruity not lost on Tess who sometimes developed the warning signs of a weak ticker when she was around Margot—the tingling of regret, the hardening of pride. But she loved her daughter fiercely and leaned down to kiss her forehead.

"It can be complicated, exes and steps and all that," Tess said. A long marriage had buffered her from the things her divorced friends had had to contend with, stepchildren whose overnight bags held not only pajamas but also other women's contempt. "You get used to life being unpredictable with kids. In other words, plan nothing." She laughed. Or plan everything, Tess wanted to add, just so you'll remember how you once imagined your life was going to go, even hour by hour.

Margot stood and looked at the wet spot she'd left on the quilt. "It's weird, you being here without Dad. I wish he'd come too." She paused. "It's like he's dead."

"That seems a little overblown," Tess said. "You know he had to work. The world of the paper box beckons." Her daughter could take away her breath like no one else, and then leave her gasping. Dead? How could she tell her now about the split? Later, she thought, I'll tell her later. She extracted the salami from her bag.

Margot smiled and held it to her nose like a flower. "You're the only mother I know who travels with a salami."

"And don't you forget it," Tess said, and kissed her daughter again. She tasted of chlorine. On the other side of the wall, Tess heard Kirk urging his little soldier, his ghostly comrade, to join him for a soak.

When the others had gone for an afternoon ski, Tess stared at the shaved pudendum of the mountain through binoculars. She tried to spot Margot in the red suit she'd vacuum-sealed herself into, etching her way down the slope. Tess didn't get the appeal of skiing, had never believed in the heroism of wind-burned faces and the bravado of broken bones. For years, she'd watched her family get expensively whisked up mountains, and she'd felt only grateful for the solid ground under her boots, though she'd sometimes imagined Ben flying off the gondola or a ledge just for his supposed fun. She wandered around the house, noting evidence of Kirk's first family everywhere, as if they had only gone out for a while; the ugly duck motif in the kitchen, the dusty, funereal silk flowers in a mug on the back of the toilet, a flannel dog bed when there clearly was no dog anymore. And of course, the boy, the palest evidence of all. At lunch, he hadn't been allowed salami or nuts, or ketchup, or strawberries, or chocolate—there was an exhaustive list on the fridge—and he had pushed around his crustless white-bread and butter sandwich. Behind Kirk's coaxing him to eat, Tess had picked up the man's deep fear of his kid. She knew it all too well. It wasn't hard for children to find exactly where their power lay with their parents and pitch their tent there.

Tess went to her room and unfolded herself on the bed. What she wanted now, in order to fight off a mid-afternoon sleep, was to recall that weekend in Millboro, but getting there meant pushing aside books and boxes, battered cake pans and old coats, her kids' artwork and sneakers and medical records, the dusty impulses of a long marriage. There'd been an old Cape house, a pond crowned by cattails, and a clipped field that ran up to a line of mountains, wooden chairs that sank into the ground as the evenings went on. There'd been that shit, Gerald, Eli's new friend and fascination that summer, and Gerald's girlfriend, a beautiful, studious woman, entirely nameless now. The pictures came to Tess in disorganized snaps, which was the closest she could come to describing what middle age was really like. The past was all there still, but you weren't sure how to organize it anymore into a story that made sense.

After dinner, Kirk massaged his wide lower back and traced on the dark window the way he'd come down the mountain earlier. Tess liked him enough, she decided, though she might not be hard pressed to admit that he was a blowhard. He was rich from commercial real estate, and apparently nothing was prettier to him than a building's empty shell. She told him about the abandoned dress shop near her office, and how the sun passed through in the mornings like a nurse visiting the terminal ward. A dress shop? He didn't get what she was talking about, or why she found the decline both sad and beautiful. Margot, reading *Newsweek,* likely understood all too well her mother's romantic notions and dismissed them. Standing at the cold glass, Tess began to understand why her daughter had married Kirk and married so young. He was a perfectly uncomplicated refuge, a little dull and dense. And yet, there was the most complicated boy in this picture Margot had also gotten in the deal, who, next to Kirk's fleshy finger reflected on the window, was curled on the couch. His knees were pulled up to his chin.

"You OK, Ry?" Kirk asked. He leaned over his son but kept his hands behind his back. Patterns of gas flames from the fireplace played over the boy's face. "All right?"

Tess put her palm against Ryan's forehead. His eyes squeezed as if her touch hurt. "He is a little hot."

"Because he's in front of the fire," Margot said. Her tone was unlovely. "He's fine."

Kirk looked from child to wife to child to wife, an unconfident volley. Tess sat next to the boy. It had been years since she'd felt the perfect heft of a child's head in her lap. She couldn't say she felt affection for him exactly at that moment, the warmth of his skin against her palm, but the kid who wasn't loveable was the one you had to go all out for. The love was sludgier, richer maybe. She looked down into the shiny spiral of the boy's ear. What's in there, she wondered, who's home? Soon Kirk scooped up the boy and carried him to the sleeping loft.

Margot closed her magazine. "Ryan makes himself sick, you know."

"Come on," Tess said. "Children don't do that. They can't."

Margot leaned forward to whisper. "He goes over to another kid's house and he gets sick, and on field trips, and at school so he has to be sent home. And sometimes when he's with us. Kirk doesn't see it."

"Maybe the boy just wants the world to stop for him until he figures it out," Tess said. "He seems lost. He needs love in the meantime." In the silence, she knew she'd angered Margot. After all, they were not talking about Ben, as Margot would point out. History was not reruns.

"I try," Margot said. "I really do. It's not easy."

The admission astonished Tess, and she considered that maybe she didn't know Margot as well as she thought she did. Wasn't that part of her family's problem, that they were all stuck in their old stories? Margot might well understand about the split, after all; she had grown up some. They averted their eyes from each other and listened to Kirk pleading with the boy to get into his pajamas; Tess imagined it could go on forever, and the boy might still prevail. It depressed her. She kissed Margot goodnight and went downstairs to her bedroom. She fell easily into the tropics of sleep, but woke at 4:30. For a minute, she thought her bag on the opposite bed was Eli, zipped up with everything familiar stuffed inside. She could open it, root around in the contents, but still wouldn't know what she was looking for. Or she could ask, *are you awake, E? Are we really doing this? I'm terrified.* She yanked the bag to the floor. Someone was walking around upstairs, thwacking the refrigerator door shut, and then it was quiet, but she knew she wasn't going back to sleep. She didn't mind how this early waking could make her day endless, but she wasn't always prepared for how possibility suggested itself to her as a naked proposal in the light of these uncertain hours. It had been possible, she'd discovered at a time just like this, to consider the end of her marriage. Ben had exhausted everything. It had seemed possible to have the half of life left to her feel like something that could be whole again.

She put on her bathrobe. The hot tub moaned under its plastic blanket as she passed. Upstairs, she looked at the mountain. Machines zigzagged across its face as showers of manufactured snow caught in the orange headlights. She heard the steady mouth-breathing of the boy above her in the loft. It was on her way back to her room that she saw him asleep on the kidney-shaped dog bed in the corner of the kitchen. He fit perfectly on the flannel, hands balled under his chin, tail tucked between his legs.

The morning was sunny and punctuated with the staccato of things dripping, which apparently was not great skiing news for Kirk, who appeared after breakfast in his obscene tube of ski clothing. He went out to pack up the car, but Tess sensed there was something else besides irritation over slope conditions going on, that his exit and Margot's position at the head of the table were planned. Her daughter fiddled with the uneaten triangles of Ryan's toast.

Tess opened a decade-old Vermont tourist brochure she'd found in the downstairs bathroom and tapped at a faded picture. "While you're skiing, I'm going to see the world's largest frozen waterfall," she said.

Margot gave the page a cursory look and then they both turned to watch Kirk load up the car. "I have a favor to ask. Ryan doesn't feel well. Will you stay with him while we go skiing?"

"You know he slept on the dog bed last night?"

"We'll just be gone a few hours. Back after lunch."

"A dog bed, Margot. The boy slept on the dog bed." Tess wasn't sorry to see Kirk, the fugitive father, slip and land on his ass as a pair of skis slid down the driveway. "Did you hear me?"

"I heard you, but what can I do? He likes it," Margot said. "I made his lunch. Put him in front of the TV or he won't eat. And don't let him have chocolate. You know where the list of bad food is, right? Nothing but the sandwich, or he'll puke."

Ryan appeared above them, leaning on the loft's railing while earphones fed him music. His hair was a nest above a triumphant smile. The boy had it all over Margot and Kirk, had them perfectly hog-tied. Tess had to admire the way he banished them to the mountain and how he sang along to lyrics he surely didn't understand. He got what he wanted—when he had nothing he needed, it seemed. Out in the driveway, Kirk warmed up the car as the wipers swung in escape across the windshield.

Pitterpat Flow is one of the world's greatest natural wonders, Tess read in the brochure. From November to March, visitors will be able to view the miraculous power of water in its stilled state. Some fifty feet high, the Flow is a frozen picture in time.

She didn't believe a word of the hype, but was interested in the intersection—if there even was one—of the lie and the truth. She would take the kid with her, and when she was ready to go, she climbed the ladder to the loft. On the bed, amid a sea of clothes and babyish stuffed animals, was the boy with his headphones still on. His eyes were closed as he played with his stiff little penis. She gulped with amusement, and some small measure of embarrassment. Why bother the kid now?

On the other hand, she thought, he can give it up for a while and we can make something of the day. She rattled the ladder, and soon he appeared at the top. "Get dressed," she said, motioning him to take off his earphones. "I'm taking you to see one of the world's greatest natural wonders."

His expression hinted at a challenge. "I can't go. I'm sick."

"Even sick people can go. Especially sick people. Says so in the brochure. Do you need help getting dressed?"

He waved her away and soon reappeared in the clothes he'd worn the day before, the white turtleneck with its timeline of purloined food. She helped zip up his awful lavender puffy boots. Girls' boots, she decided; his mother wasn't helping matters. The boy was fidgety in the car and it occurred to her that he should probably be in the back given his weight, but she didn't move him. She was beginning to like his strange presence next to her. She told him they were going to see a frozen waterfall.

Ryan opened and closed the heating vents. "If it's a waterfall, it's moving, so it can't be frozen," he said.

"Ah, smarty-pants, the brochure says differently. And I believe everything I read, don't you?"

"Do you have a husband?" he asked.

"Yes, his name is Eli. He couldn't come because he had to work."

"I'm hungry."

This struck her as a perfectly reasonable response. She realized that she'd forgotten the prescribed sandwich. Maybe she could find something harmless for him; mashed potatoes, oatmeal, a banana, saltines, snow. Foods that matched his color. She gave him an Altoid, which he spit into his mitten with great drama. Soon she took a road that ran parallel to the highway. On either side were fields of untouched snow, a few houses set far back. Occasional buildings appeared, signs of life, but no actual life itself. The Family Restaurant turned out, despite its benign name and frilly curtains, to not be a particularly homey place, the bell on the door signaling the few people nursing coffee to look up and stare. The boy took a booth facing the sanded lot.

"Bacon cheeseburger with french fries and a coke," Ryan announced to the waitress and slapped his plastic menu shut. "And that will do it."

Tess laughed at his swagger. She considered overruling his order, just in case, but in the end, she asked for the same, though she wasn't hungry. "You're a funny guy," she told him. "Do you know that?"

He asked her for a pen and began to scribble on the placemat that advertised local businesses: a maple sugar museum, the birthplace of M. Cotter.

"You're not really my grandmother," Ryan said, his pen obliterating the Tru-Value logo.

"That's half true. I'm your step-grandmother. My daughter is your stepmother."

He looked up. "Who's your daughter?"

"Margot." Her water tasted as though it had been pulled right from the frozen ground. "Remember? She's married to your father."

"I know that." He rolled his eyes and sighed. "Stupid lady."

Had she expected him to like her because she was the champion of troubled boys everywhere? She felt stung. Their food arrived with lettuce and tomato that Ryan dropped on the table. He concentrated on the descent of ketchup from the bottle, and when too much flooded the meat, he removed the sludge with a finger that he then wiped down the front of his shirt. Tess pushed a napkin toward him. He ate in feral bites, pushing in the fries. A single red spot pulsed in each cheek. Ketchup, a particular poison. God, what else? Why had she let him do this? To prove that none of it was true? A cold flow of worry ran through her.

"I'm done," he said, and pushed his plate away. "I have to pee."

He slid out of the booth. People at the counter watched him because he was, in his own way, entirely unforgettable, a little boy, a shrunken old man. Tess looked out onto the parking lot just as a filthy crust of snow fell off her back fender. The sun was high and thin; she could almost imagine spring here, waiting in this booth for it to arrive. She took out her cell phone and called Eli. She wanted to tell him where she was and who she was with, but she was dumped to his voice mail. Splitting up had not been his idea, and it had taken her forever to convince him that it was what they both wanted and needed, that Ben had left them worn out. Eli fought and his fury was a lightning storm. And then he called her from work one day to say OK, and behind him she heard the clatter of the folding machines; he'd chosen to talk to her from the factory floor with its well-tuned industry, its loyalty and agency, its perfume of glue and cardboard dust. She'd spent half her life there too. Decorative paper boxes; it was what the world needed, they'd discovered together. She didn't expect now to feel such regret, but she missed him with an ache.

Ryan had been in the bathroom too long. If he didn't come out in a minute, she'd have to get him. And if he wasn't all right? The waitress came over to take their plates.

"Are we close to Pitterpat Flow?" Tess asked her.

The girl had never heard of the place, nor had the two men sitting at the counter, but there was only one road it could be on—and Tess was on it. She felt oddly conspired against, as though they were leading her down a dark alley. Ryan appeared with the triumphant, feel-good look of a boy who has pumped the soap dispenser a few thousand times and pulled a few hundred towels from the silver box. The front of his shirt was wet, plastered against his thin chest and sesame seed nipples. He'd tried to scrub off the ketchup.

Outside, the temperature had dropped, and in the car, the boy slipped inside the warm nest of his coat. They passed the occasional yard sale, sleds and skis stuck into the snow like athletic grave markers. Set back on the left side of the road was a deserted hut with a faded sign for Pitterpat Flow. The lot was unplowed, the structure an unreachable artifact and she drove past. She imagined plaits of ice, the relic of a faster fall. That would have to do. She couldn't imagine the trek through the snow and leaving the evidence of her footprints.

"I have to pee," Ryan said.

"Listen," Tess said. "I know all about little boys and their needing to pee. You just went; you can hold it now."

But he wiggled and thumped at his crotch until Tess stopped. He wouldn't go in the open, though they had yet to see another person, and insisted on climbing into the thickness of the woods. Tess followed his sickly purple boots and turned away from the sight of his pants pulled down and his bare white bottom. She wondered if his father had ever taught him a single, useful thing. The air was sharp with balsam and alive with the soft plop of falling pine cones. She stood where the woods ended above a field, dried stalks punching up through the snow in cold protest, and in the distance, a series of red barns and outbuildings. This was the goat farm Gerald had walked them to one afternoon that weekend. She recalled the organic odor and how Eli had been too embarrassed to milk a goat. She had found her way into Millboro; she'd wanted to see it again, and why not? She was allowed; it wasn't a bad thing to remember. A rumble made her turn to spot the purple boots and the boy struggling with his pants, and then back to see a line of snowmobiles plowing through the field.

The procession bounced and zipped and flew. It looked exhilarating. The boy galloped up to her.

"I missed them," he cried. His face was twisted with despair now that the caravan had slid into the distance. "Shitting fucker. Shitting, shitting fucker."

"You'll get other chances, I promise," she said, but he was as despondent as an ancient emperor. "You have to move quickly when you hear them. You'll think you have forever, but then they're gone."

He stomped back to the car, still swearing. Did he always get what he wanted? His disappointment was palpable and adult. Tess drove by the goat farm and toward where she thought the house had been. Ryan said she was driving in the wrong direction and shook his head like an irked spouse. The curve was too long, and what appeared first was the Blue Wales Motel that had been under construction back then. The place had an old face now, the shutters drooping with palsy. Gerald had wanted Eli to invest in it with him, but Eli's money and her own was already in the box business. Gerald had said that Eli was too young to be so tied up and tied down, his balls in a vice. Eli had given her, his new wife, a contrite look.

"I've been here before," she told Ryan, who claimed he felt sick. Tess put her hand on his forehead. "You shouldn't say you're sick if you're not. When you really are sick, no one will believe you."

"I almost died once," he said. Her hand was still on his forehead. "When I was born, I had to stay in the hospital for a long time. I couldn't eat because I threw up everything. I was this tiny little guy who almost died for days and days and days."

You were this tiny little guy who almost died. She could hear the line being told over and over. This is what families did—they turned their lowest moments into stories to live off, to mark their survival by. Remember the window Ben smashed, remember Margot's bloody nose and the raw scratch down her back, remember the stunning ferocity her children had brought out in each other, the violence they inflicted.

"But you're not going to die now," she said. "That was a long time ago, and now you're fine. Healthy and very, very smart. I think you have great powers."

"Bullshit," he announced, but smiled.

Farther down the road was the same white Cape house with the mountains as backdrop. Gerald had wanted to buy the place, but she didn't imagine for a second that he actually had. Bullies didn't win. She pulled up in front. The door was open as a woman tried to push a reluctant cat out with her foot. When she saw Tess' car, she used her book as a visor and squinted into the white distance. The cat squeezed back inside. Tess thought about driving away.

"Are you looking for something?" the woman yelled. The cold thinned her voice. "Are you lost?"

It was Poppy, Gerald's girlfriend. Gone for years and that red, sexy name was there instantly. The shock of seeing her was like seeing the actual flower in the snow. Tess had assumed that Gerald and Poppy had split up at the end of the summer.

"Tell her no," Ryan whispered.

Tess leaned out. "My husband was a friend of Gerald's. Eli. Eli and Tess? From a long time ago?"

Wind rolled across the snow banks, whitening the air and the retrieval of memories. "Eli and Tess? From a hundred years ago? My god, come in." She waved with her book. "Come in!"

"I don't want to," Ryan insisted. He pressed a hand over his stomach. "I don't feel good."

"Remember? You're fine. There's nothing wrong with you."

He scuffed up the front walk behind her. Poppy was still beautiful, half-gray now, still had the longest legs. Glasses hung from a beaded string. The intervening years did not for one second lessen Tess' notion that Poppy was another species of woman—elegant, desirable, emotionally impractical. She felt wan and generic next to her, just as Eli had appeared solid and stiff next to Gerald's lean and hectic height. Poppy and Gerald had been a magnificent-looking couple. Gerald had gone without a shirt much of the hot weekend, enormously strong, exuding conquest and a smell of sex and sweat. Tess had been overheated with erotic envy.

"We can't come in," Tess said. She didn't want to see Gerald. "I just wanted to say hello."

But Poppy insisted as she looked at Ryan and absently touched a small diamond in her ear. A woman without children, Tess decided, a woman all to herself. They shed their coats and boots, but there was nowhere to leave soggy clothing, not on the pristine Shaker bench that held a stack of books and a wine-colored leather bag. Tess' damp socks left prints on the bleached floor, but to take them off seemed too intimate. Already she was stalling—why had she agreed to come in anyway? Her attachment to the past struck her as dangerous. Now and then was likely to slam shut and she'd be caught in the middle, her fingers squeezed in the hinges.

The kitchen was no longer cramped, but airy with a full wall of windows that looked out onto the field silvered with mist and the pond with its fringe of reeds. Gerald got just what he wanted: the house, the woman. Poppy's brilliant green eyes had only faded a little. And Tess, so smug in her marriage that ancient weekend, was the one driving around now like someone who was entirely lost.

"Amazing." Poppy turned the gas on under the kettle. "After all this time. There are people you imagine you'll never see again, and then you do. And it just blows you away."

"I'm surprised you remember me," Tess said.

"But you remembered me, didn't you?" She glanced at Ryan on his stomach in front of the fire. The cat slithered around his head. "Life gallops—children with children—while it still feels like last summer. God, I sound like an old lady." They laughed companionably.

Where do we begin? Tess wondered. She took the cup of tea Poppy offered. She'd begin at the end—today. There was the goat farm, the frozen falls, her son-in-law's house, her daughter, the boy who wasn't really her grandson.

"And Eli?" Poppy asked, tentatively.

"Eli's fine." Tess looked into the pale brown water in her cup. "So Gerald actually bought this place. He always struck me as the kind of man who would get everything he wanted in life."

Poppy smiled. "Not at all. This is my house. I've had it for almost fifteen years. I come up from the city when I can." Her eyes cinched at the corners. "Gerald died. You knew that, didn't you?"

Tess had been picturing someone who didn't exist.

"I hadn't talked to him in years," Poppy explained. "We were married for one, divorced forever. I always felt bad about that weekend. Gerald was a fool, his own enemy. He thought people were behind him, when really they were much farther ahead."

Tess didn't think Poppy knew that the men had fought.

"How did he die?"

"Fell off a ladder. It would have killed him to know that something so banal did him in." Poppy seemed embarrassed by her own smile.

Tess looked at Ryan. She had an impulse to pull him onto her lap. There was the familiar drone of snowmobiles and a line of them appeared from the left. They edged the pond on the far side before they disappeared. Digging above Ryan's upper lip was the disappointment that she'd failed once again to call him in time. Having dashed to the window, he now showed her his bottom teeth like a dog.

"I hate those things," Poppy said. "If I could, I'd buy the land and keep them off with a shotgun." She let her head fall to the side and she pushed around the skin on the back of her hand.

"We should get going," Tess said.

Poppy hated to ask, but would Tess help her with something outside before they left? She opened a closet stuffed with winter gear, the browns of men's coats, enormous boots, gloves for working hands. There had been men in the house, some Poppy might have loved, but none who remained. Poppy handed Tess a pair of heavy socks. The cold was alarming, the sun falling fast over a path tamped down in the snow that led to a small shed. Poppy had been trying to work the door open and get to the firewood, but had managed only to pound the snow against itself into an immoveable icy wedge. It would have been better to dig in the first place, but it was too late now. The small ineptitude of a woman living alone surprised Tess.

Poppy's breath came out in pink, determined clouds as they rocked the door back and forth. Tess smelled the lichened wood inside, and saw through the inches of open door, seams of light falling over the logs. Gerald had told Eli that Poppy was sexually uptight, that he was going to dump her at the end of the summer because he needed someone who could really fuck. Eli, furious, told Tess this in their bedroom across the hall from where Gerald and Poppy slept. She was struck by how innocent her husband was in some ways and how the look into others' lives made them both self-conscious. They didn't know anything about fucking. The next morning they'd watched Poppy, breezy in a sleeveless dress, scrambling eggs, while Gerald ground into her from behind. Poppy had leaned back, her spatula poised. Eli had watched them too. She wished now that she'd asked him what he'd been thinking and that she might have known her husband best in that moment.

"Gerald was a bastard," Tess said.

Poppy stopped pulling on the door. "No, that weekend, maybe. I think Eli brought something out in him, some kind of panic or competition probably."

"He said not nice things about you."

"Oh, he was always saying something awful about everyone. He thought it was motivating." Poppy seemed cautious, her gaze far off, and Tess knew she shouldn't say anymore. "Don't tell me, ok? I don't want to know what he said." Poppy shook her head. "Shit. I can't believe I'm crying."

"I'm sorry. I don't know why I even brought it up."

"It's ok. It's just that I haven't thought of him in a long time, that's all." She shook her head and led them back to the house.

Tess would have liked to sit down for a minute, but Poppy didn't take off her coat and told Tess to keep the socks. She was clearly ready for them to leave. But Ryan was not in front of the fire. His boots and coat were still in the hall and he was not upstairs. Tess looked at the field and saw the last sunlight gild footsteps toward the pond.

She heard the noise and saw the snowmobiles' lights cut through the cold. She knew the boy wouldn't let himself miss another chance to see them. She ran through the snow with her feet barely rising above the winter line. Poppy was behind her somewhere, saying something, asking something. The boy wasn't smart. He was scared to death of himself. He would be struck, tossed into the air, and struck by another machine down the line. She was a careless, breathless woman and he was the color of the snow, an endless season, a sun always hidden behind clouds. Who would believe this was how both their lives would end?

She fell back into the reeds. The purpling sky rose above her. The machines passed and faded into ribbons, and then she heard sounds of absolute, exhilarating pleasure from the boy. He'd made a seat for himself in the reeds where he was close enough to smell the fumes and have the snow spit on his face. He was enthralled, his body pulsing with excitement. Tess turned to Poppy who stood to her left. At first Tess thought she was meant to take the offered hand, but when she stood, Poppy slapped her hard across the face. For a moment Poppy froze, and then she ran back to the house. Tess didn't feel anything, but she thought she might shatter.

"Did you see?" the boy asked. His face was wet with snow. "I saw the machines. I saw them close."

At the house, Tess sat the boy on the bench and told him not to move. She went upstairs to find Poppy. Her cheek burned; she'd apologize. She looked into the room where she and Eli had slept. On their last night, Eli's disappointment in Gerald was suffocating. She'd woken to the sound of the men outside and looked down at them through the bars of the headboard. Gerald was naked, his chest luminous, his penis thick, Eli in shorts that cut into his unyielding waist. Eli swung ambitiously at Gerald who stumbled back, then forward, and landed one in return. One thrown punch each, then they were done, stepping back, hands up in truce. Not fighters really, but they wouldn't ever talk again.

Poppy appeared in the doorway. "I hit you."

"You were scared. It's OK."

"I'm not apologizing." Her hands were in her sweater pockets. "I wasn't expecting any of this. I didn't invite it. Would you leave now?"

Poppy went downstairs first and stood at the open door, indifferent to the cold air rushing in, and Tess and Ryan rushing out.

It was dark now, hours late, and Tess pulled into the Blue Wales lot to call Margot and Kirk. Margot would have called her father already, furious and worried, and Eli might have broken the news. But she couldn't find her phone, not in the yellowed light of the car's interior, and she knew it could be anywhere really, on the Family Restaurant's sticky seat or in Poppy's field. Ryan, sated with excitement, had fallen asleep. The fake fur of his hood moved with his breath, and tiny beads of moisture caught on the fiber's ends.

Tess drove too fast and the car swerved on patches of ice. Thirty minutes later, idling on the side of the road in front of Pitterpat Flow was Margot and Kirk's car. Tess pulled up behind it. She would apologize; no harm done, except some worry, but for that she was very sorry. She knew what it was like to worry. She left the car running and got out. The suv's tinted windows were infuriating, prolonging the freeze as she stood there like a penitent. She clicked the glass with her ring. The window went down to reveal not Kirk, as she'd expected, but her daughter, alone.

"Where have you been?" Margot demanded. She pressed her temples with the heels of her hands. "Is he ok?"

"He's fine." The air was perfect now, a cold silver string.

"That's it? That's all you're going to say? He's fine?"

The day she and Eli had taken Ben to Alsop, Margot had waited on the steps of the house with this same rage when they returned. "Where is my brother? Where did you take him?" she'd asked. Tess hadn't heard her daughter's fear then, but she heard it now. Fear and some kind of difficult love in that rage. Tess moved the boy to Margot's car. She told her daughter that she'd been to the place, even the room, where Margot had first been imagined, an amazing thing after Eli's fistfight. An amazing thing now on this foreign, snow-bound road, but Margot was saying something to the boy, leaning over him, her face hidden in the depths of his hood, and she didn't hear her mother.

GARY FINCKE

At Midnight, On My Birthday

My mother, dead at my age, unclasps
her beaded purse as if entering
my house requires a ticket.

For twenty-one years, she says,
she's carried the proper ID
for pain, waiting to hand it over.

She's dreamed my body
crippled in yesterday's underwear,
my breath caught in phlegm's thick web.

In a doubled brown paper sack,
she's brought twelve pounds of pennies
gathered from sidewalks and carpets.

She asks me to arrange them in rolls
for the teller she knows by name,
the woman who lost her husband

at Normandy. She shakes my clipped hair
and nails from her purse, spelling my name
with her finger in the thick dust of me.

Only after she knows the exact sum
of her savings does she allow me
to moan my symptoms. Lie down, she says,

so I can love you. In two places,
she ties her green gown behind me.
There, she says, now finish undressing.

And yes, she examines me,
saying, "Relax now, close your eyes.
This is where the past ends."

RITA ANN HIGGINS
His Brazen Hair

I was looking at the Brian Bourke exhibition
in the Fairgreen Gallery.
Outside, a man lay collapsed on the ground.
It was freaking people out
they kept coming in telling the person
at the desk about the man on the ground.

After a while the guards came,
they were wearing blue gloves.
They knew the body on the ground.
They poked him with the blue gloves.
Get up Gerry, get up outta that.

Don't you know
there's an exhibition on in there Gerry
and you are making a right exhibition
outta yourself out here.

Gerry didn't you know the Arts festival was on
he didn't know about Brian Bourke's nudes.
Otherwise he might have washed his face
patted down his brazen hair
pulled himself together.

JONATHAN JOHNSON
Out Far Enough

For sorrow we have love and the waves dying in.

We can visit our lives in the country of winter trees and blue ruin.

For the nameless we have silence.

Where tenderness runs out there is tenderness.

A trail descends into the next glen.

Our anti-muse's hair is the color of loam.

For gospel she has shelved volumes of everything we leave unwritten.

For forgiveness she has light from a peat fire, rain on small windows.

SHAENA LAMBERT
The War Between the Men and the Women

It was 1968 and there was a war between the men and the women.
Jane heard it on the radio, where for the first time women's voices
read the news; and she saw it at school, where her art teacher, Miss
Hannah Shapiro, had started going braless—great wandering breasts
shifting this way and that under soft denim; and there it was, on the
bus: women traveling into Vancouver from the islands displayed gloms
of hair beneath their arms.

At home, things were still as a knife blade. Her father sliced the ham,
laying a piece on Jane's plate, while Gretchen, Jane's mother, watched
from her end of the table, wary and silent. Jane sat between them. She
had the same foxy coloring as her father; the same sharp eyes and sandy
lashes. She looked like a different race from her slender, bangled mother.

The curtains blocked out the back of Hollyburn Mountain.
The neighborhood dogs had been called in. Children were at their
homework, or television, or sitting down to eat, though few followed
such perverse rituals: three-course meals with salad, ham and vegetables,
dessert. Wine, some even poured for Jane. Even before things got bad,
Jane felt like a chained dog, wanting to run around the table, wolf her
food, bite someone's leg off. Anything to stop this nightly ritual.

The overhead light cast its glow.

Patrick's pointed chin was hidden but not forgotten beneath a trim
beard. He wore a flannel shirt, over which he had donned a sweater
vest. He never wanted to turn the heat up. As for Gretchen, doling out
the scalloped potatoes, the only trace of her subversion was in the color
of her hands. Tonight her skin had turned crimson, with Prussian blue
in the veins.

While Patrick was teaching at the university, Gretchen was in the
shed dyeing cloth, coating it with wax, cracking the wax to let the dye
seep through, and then hanging lengths from the clothesline, where
they dripped ruby blood onto the grass. Then she showered, changed,
applied makeup, and waited for the rev of Patrick's MG up the driveway.

"How was your lecture on Hannibal?" she asked.

You could tell he had been waiting for this moment, ever since getting home: just look at the need on his face. The martini and wine hadn't hurt, either, causing a slow emanation of dissatisfaction, like gas released from a chasm in the earth.

Yes, the students had received his annual lecture on the Second Punic War. No, they had not been inordinately impressed. They had shuffled papers. They had coughed. They had asked the inane questions they always asked. He had responded in Latin to flummox them, to make them feel the whip of his brain on their idiots' flesh. He had told them that everything—everything—would be on the test, even the quotes he dropped in class, and that the tests themselves would come out of nowhere, like hailstorms.

"They have no conception of the challenges."

"I'm sure they don't." A murmur like a ripple in a stream.

Jane would like to put a fork through his head.

Tonight, Gretchen seemed lighter than on other nights, less absorbed in the game, and Jane knew why. She had decided to enter one of her batiks in a juried craft show in North Vancouver. Now, as she nibbled the cheese-crusted potatoes, she carried this knowledge like a bubble of mirth.

"It was merely the greatest ambush in military history," Patrick continued: "Hannibal crossing the Alps, rising out of the mist, surprising Flaminius at Lago Trasimeno. But do these students care? Half of them are on acid. The other half want classes to be held on the beach."

Jane knew the story of Hannibal's ambush. Roman legions straggling along the shore at dawn, their lines dishevelled. Near the top of a far hill they could see the glow of Hannibal's camp fires. The creak of war wagons. The smell of fear in the horses' nostrils.

"Then Hannibal's men burst out of the forest behind them. Thirty thousand Romans caught without their armor, cut down where they stood. Three hours was all it took—a single morning. Tell me this is not amazing!"

(This is not amazing, Jane thought.)

"The rivers turned red with the blood. They named towns after the bones and skeletons. Even today, farmers unearth collar bones, thigh bones, bits of armor."

Gretchen looked up. Once upon a time she had a braid stretching all the way to the small of her back, but now her hair was cut in shag. The mole on her cheek was fingerprint size, and when Jane was little she liked to put her finger over it. Her eyes were deep brown, almost black, like the mouse in Jane's old school reader. She smiled bountifully at them both, holding a piece of ham on her fork like a lollipop. "To me," she said, "it isn't actually about Hannibal at all. Or Scipio Africanus, or Flavius."

"Gaius Flaminius Nepos."

"The story—"

"It's not a *story.*"

"The history, then. It's not about the generals. Or even the dead—"

"*Ossaia, Sanguineto, Caparossa, Pugnano.*"

"I see it all," Gretchen straightened her back, "from the elephants' perspective."

Jane laughed.

"Imagine," Gretchen lowered her voice, "how shocked they must have been, coming from Africa, across the Mediterranean, shaken back and forth in the hold of a boat. Then up, over the Alps and what do they see? Snow!"

"They must have been freezing," said Jane.

"Nothing prepared them. Though perhaps an old elephant—some elephant guru two hundred years before—had foretold the catastrophe, passing down the knowledge from elephant to elephant: 'a day will come, my children, when the sky will turn white and fall to earth in little pieces.'"

Patrick watched his wife carefully. "*Ex Africa semper aliquid novi.*"

"They must have gotten frostbite on their feet."

"Thirty thousand Romans caught without their armor."

"The skin of the elephants turned milky in the moonlight."

Patrick pushed scalloped potatoes onto his upturned fork. A pea rolled away but was captured. "But why stop there, my love? Why not see it from the perspective of the camp dogs?"

"Why not, indeed."

"Or the cockroaches. Or the maggots. This is only the greatest military tragedy in history that you're ridiculing. In fact," he placed his napkin by his plate, "you could be one of my students, because this is what I put up with all day." Before Gretchen could speak again, Patrick stood. "The potatoes were oversalted," he said, "and you, my love, have had too much to drink." Then he was gone, to watch the television news downstairs.

Jane kept her head down, examining her plate, which was stoneware with flecks across the surface like faraway birds. Gretchen began to clear the plates, pausing to press a hot palm to Jane's forearm. Jane brushed it away. After a moment she heard Gretchen moving in the kitchen, ankle bracelet chiming like a lament.

Jane, Gretchen, and Patrick. They were conjoined like the Holy Trinity, but with Patrick always on top, interpreting the world for them, which was ridiculous, because Jane could clearly see that her mother was the deeper one. When a hollow ache woke Jane at night, a fear of death that threatened to swallow her whole, only Gretchen knew the cure: she lay down, holding Jane's body with the length of her own, in her nightgown with its ribbon of apricot satin at the neckline, which left marks on Jane's cheek. Linked hands. Linked fingers. Said these words: life will feel very long. And slowly, with the pressure of palm on palm, fingers enmeshed, smells—yeasty, earthy—rising from her mother's skin and hair, Gretchen made even the wild abyss of death disappear.

She also had subtler talents, which Jane did not wholly understand or respect.

After Patrick flounced from the table, Jane pushed back her chair and went into the kitchen. Why, she wanted to know, did Gretchen let Patrick pronounce on everything that way? Why must the conversation *always* be about his work? And what about the elephants? Did Gretchen actually care about them—their hoary frozen toes, their terrible fate tumbling from Alpine cliffs, legs chained together—or was she just pretending?

"Why does this *always* happen?"

Gretchen closed the refrigerator. Her eyes, meeting Jane's, were watery, humiliated, and for a moment Jane saw, really *saw*, that her mother did not have an answer.

"It's hard to understand when you're young."

"Yes, it is."

Once, when Jane was much younger, Patrick asked her (again this was at the dinner table) to name which of her parents she loved more. Could this be true? It felt less like a memory than like the fraught opening scenes of a Greek tragedy, or a dream where everything spins calmly out of control. Jane remembered dancing around the table, grasping her mother's braid like a bell pull, and giving it a mean tug. When Gretchen threw her wine glass against the wall and ran to the bathroom, Patrick shrugged sheepishly. "I think," he murmured, "we went too far."

Oh, they had made Jane complicit, an actor in their drama, the hair-puller! And that was what burnt later. Even two decades later, remembering those dinnertime scenes, Jane could feel the anger burning in her throat. It really shocked her, how out of control her parents had been, that was the truth of it: the lust for revenge, the poke and thrust, the sorrow.

Of course, she had to remind herself, it had been another age. 1968. Spontaneity was queen. Women screamed and hurled china. Men got drunk and groped their students. Children threw themselves from the cliffs at Lighthouse Park, landing ramrod straight in the churning water. Everybody wanted things. Everybody asked and dug and jabbed and screamed—got stoned, got drunk: wanted.

But now the Age of Aquarius was over, and a new age had been ushered in: the Age of Boundaries. If Bruce, Jane's partner, wanted to discuss their relationship, he arranged a meeting. He called her on the telephone, or told her over supper that he had things he needed to discuss (and she would do the same), and then they would arrange a sitter for three-year-old Cara and go to a coffee shop, or a wine bar, agendas in hand, and talk over their difficulties, carefully employing noninflammatory language.

Bruce was a scientist, a geologist. Once he had caught hold of Jane's system of conflict resolution, he stuck to it with a rigor that verged, Jane occasionally thought, on the punitive.

Bruce's specialty as a geologist was the Niagara Escarpment. It seemed that some of the oldest trees in the world lived on the escarpment, holding on by their roots to pockets of soil compacted in the cliff walls. Some trees were over one thousand years old but only four feet tall. Some—the most gnarled and picturesque—were in danger from bonsai poachers.

Although, like Jane, Bruce worked for the University of Toronto, he headed out each morning wearing hiking boots and with a pack on his back, looking a bit like Charlie Brown (perhaps because of his round head, which made him look young, even in his late thirties). They were both, Jane and Bruce, ginger-haired and blue-eyed, a fact that embarrassed Jane. She hoped people didn't think they had chosen each other for that reason.

Jane was a historian in the Women's Studies Department. She focused on the Neolithic matriarchal societies (partnership models, she called them) of Anatolia and Thrace, which had been subjugated by waves of horsemen descending from the steppes: Kurgans (5,000 BC), Ubaids (4,000 BC), Hittites (2,000 BC), Aryans (1,000 BC). All of these destroyers had thundered down from the grasslands, brandishing swords and battle axes, worshipping gods of the sky. Jane worked hard to make the terror real for her students. Imagine, she said, you are out collecting shells, or bent over a well of indigo, and you feel the shaking of horses' hooves rising out of the ground. You run, but the chariots bear down on you with war cries and screaming, slicing of iron weapons; rape; dismemberment; your beloved son dragged behind a chariot by his hair. The Scythians, Jane told her class, attached pouches made of human faces to their reins, displaying them as trophies.

"How goes the war?" Bruce sometimes asked when she got home from work. Or: "How are things at the front?" This was a little joke they shared, after coming across a series of James Thurber cartoons in a secondhand bookstore. It was called "The War Between Men and Women," and it had really made them laugh. Line-drawn men with egg-shaped heads clubbed startled women with umbrellas. Gangs of dowagers retaliated by hurling canned goods down the aisles of the grocery store. Several women met in a lantern-lit barn to plan their next ambush. It was like World War II—that was why it was funny. WWII, waged between men and women. As though everything subverted between the sexes could be made public in the carnival of battle. Jane had photocopied the drawings and taped them to her office door, where they remained until a colleague mentioned pointedly that the cartoons didn't seem to validate women's struggle. Jane was up for tenure, so she took the drawings down.

Jane and Bruce worked at their relationship meticulously. They tried to be consistent. But still at night, sitting alone in the living room, while Bruce took his turn putting Cara to bed, Jane could feel the container of grief threatening to spill over. It wasn't anybody's fault. Certainly not Bruce's, with his openhearted kindness, his ingenuity at fixing toasters and shower rods. And she and Bruce were both proud of what they had created, proud of their dispute-resolute mechanisms, their absolute equality.

I love you, he said as he left each morning, backpack on his back.
I love you too.

She suspected that he heard, as she did, the minute leap of faith required by this litany—as though they hoped, through repetition, to fan something wilder into flame.

But back in 1968 the evenings were all sturm und drang, and Jane lay in bed picturing the elephants. They followed Hannibal over the Alps, then down the body of Italy toward Gaius Flaminius, who was about to be severely outflanked. As Jane fell asleep, the two men, one dark, one light, took hold of each other and wrestled beside the lake. Hannibal's gold earring glinted. Gaius was as skinny as a slice of moon. On they struggled, slick with oil, while behind them, with utter disregard, elephants chomped at the sweet lake grass.

When Jane cried out, Gretchen was there, blocking the hall light, lying down. To distract Jane, Gretchen sang songs or recited the kinds of fishing flies she knew how to tie—tricks her father had taught her when she was growing up on a remote lake in the Shuswaps, in the interior of the province, during the war. *Silhouetted damsels. Deer-haired nymphs. Goldenheads. Silver Doctors.* These names caused a ruckus and shine in Jane's head. She lay beside her mother, picturing that remote hunting and fishing lodge with its cook house, and eight wooden cabins with green shutters that raised and lowered on hinges. Wood stoves for heat. Four outhouses.

It wasn't a camp people brought their children to. There were just men up from the city on hunting trips, or expert fishermen or, now and then, a couple, like the honeymoon couple who came thinking the place would be romantic. The lady, bored and fretful, had tried to suntan at the end of the dock, which turned out to be impossible because of the bugs. The day before she left, she had painted all of Gretchen's toenails red.

It was Gretchen's loneliness that Jane felt, each time she heard the stories. Jane closed her eyes, and she saw her mother as a little girl running after her father through the long grass, which soaked her jeans, and this image radiated a great throb of loneliness from its center.

She saw her grandfather, Hans, pulling on his cork boots and then walking past the cabins to stand on the dock. Gretchen ran after him and slipped without a word into the bow of the rowboat. Jane imagined the thunk of the oar blade against the dock as they pushed away, shooting across the reeds. They rowed past Butterfly Cove and Mermaid Rock, toward the dark side of the lake. Hans cast and trout came to his hook, but Gretchen, age five, didn't care about the fish anymore.

"How many days?"

First it was one hundred sixteen. Then eighty-three. Then—miraculously—sixteen. Sixteen days until the end of banishment. Sixteen days until the first day of school.

Gretchen saw her father looking toward the end of the lake where the Outlier cabin sat in its private cove. One of its shutters was off kilter. He rowed into the bay, tied up to a sapling, and they went to investigate. If a wolverine had been inside, it could do serious damage. Wolverines were ferocious and carried long grudges; Gretchen could feel her father's worry. He pulled open the door, and mattress ticking floated everywhere. The bed had been knifed open, canisters overturned, bacon grease and cornmeal spread on the floor to form a messy swastika. And the worst part—someone had taken a shit on an enamel plate and left it on the card table.

As for the first day of school at Sicamous Elementary—it was inevitable—how could it not be? This little girl from the woods was bound for sorrow, just like a character in one of the folk songs Gretchen sang. No friends were going to gather around her in pastel dresses, bows in their hair: not likely. She was an enemy alien with scabbed knees and a German name, whose jacket smelled of wood smoke, whose parents couldn't afford saddle shoes. What happened next was as inevitable as coughing, as lying down, as dying—and Jane wished, whenever she heard the story, that she could go back in time, step from behind a corner of the schoolhouse, walk past the tittering girls and take her mother's hand. *I'll play with you,* is what she would say, if she had that kind of power.

But now it was 1968, and the women of West Vancouver were swollen with different longings. They tie-dyed their husbands' handkerchiefs while they were at work; they used the good silver to hot-knife hash; or, like Gretchen, they spread moonlike silk on the table in the woodshed, and prepared to make something beautiful, while in a nearby cedar a woodpecker went at the bark with hydraulic force.

On this day in April all the tulips opened at once, showing their stamens like dog penises. Jane walked home from school. She didn't like to eat in the playground, because some of the boys had named her *Gorki Pickle.* Now why had they done that? Was it her plump stomach? Red hair? White legs? Boys seemed to sense the changes in her body: breast buds, softening nipples, the arrival of foxy hair around her pubis. She smelled of sabotage.

To make matters worse, Miss Shapiro, her favorite teacher, had told the class she planned to leave school midterm, right after Easter break, in order to travel to Mexico. She used the term, *find herself*— she wanted to *find herself* in Mexico—inspiring Jane with the cloudy understanding that one's self could actually go missing. And suppose (this was what Patrick said later, when he heard), suppose Miss Shapiro went to Acapulco, but her self was in Puerto Vallarta.

Jane opened the back gate, tuna sandwich in one hand. The yard smelled of wood bugs and mulch, a leafy scent of decay. The shed door was open and Gretchen was singing. She had a good voice, mellow and low, and Jane, stepping along the gravel path, felt the song like a caress. The cedar-filled air released the boys' voices from where they had settled in her throat.

Inside the shed, Gretchen stood over a table covered by a length of white silk held along each edge with carpenter's clamps. It was taut as the skin of a drum and had a bluish cast to it. Gretchen held a tjanting in her hand—a penlike instrument with a fluted spout, out of which a line of wax could pour. The fabric lit her cheeks and forehead.

"You're home. Everything OK?"

Jane nodded. She could not say to her mother—*they call me Gorki Pickle*. She couldn't say, *I am crushed by something large on my chest*. Jane reached out a finger to touch the fabric.

"Are your hands clean? It's watered silk."

Watered silk.

"It's slippery."

"I was just about to make my first mark."

It was almost too exciting, this immortal moment, with its honey scent of beeswax and paraffin, the enamel pot bubbling on the hot plate, ready for the poisons—acid blue, mordant yellow, raw sienna. Gretchen cupped her hand beneath the tjanting and stared down at the pure swath of fabric. She cocked her head, narrowed her eyes, and something artful in this birdlike gesture made Jane suspicious. Gretchen shifted her weight, preparing to touch wax to cloth, and she seemed all at once like a puppet, pulling her own strings, radiant with the effort of making this one moment matter. What did she hope for? Jane felt an itch of irritation gather under her clothes. Only much later, as a grownup, did she understand what her mother must have needed. She wanted a ripe line of wax to flow from the tjanting, such as might come from the pen of a Zen calligrapher; thick, thin, even, uneven; pure; followed by another, and then another: moments of grace; God visiting her softly, without fuss, right there in the backyard woodshed.

That was all.

Back at school, Miss Shapiro had gone to the principal, telling him that she intended to leave at Easter break.

"You can't," he had said.

"I have to."

"Then go now. Right now." The gauntlet thrown.

When Jane entered the art room, Miss Shapiro was kneeling in front of the supply cupboard, a clutch of her favorite girls around her. She was telling them that authority did not always understand the dictates of the heart. At the same time, she was separating construction paper into two piles, as some of it was hers. One of the girls said, "Gorki Pickle, go away." But Miss Shapiro said, "Don't be ridiculous. Jane, you come and help me." And Jane stood with arms outstretched, while Miss Shapiro wound wool around her forearms.

By three o'clock Miss Shapiro was gone.

Outside, the sky had turned a darker blue. At the edge of the school parking lot, boys were throwing each other into a juniper bush, calling each other *homo,* which allowed Jane to slip by. Night hovered in the distance, hours away still, but Jane began to hurry, while also kicking a pebble with the arch of her left foot and then her right, making sure that the stone touched her shoe seam each time. A limousine was parked in the church lot, and Jane felt a wash of terror remembering the rhyme:

If you should see a hearse go by
Then you will be the next to die.

But there was nothing to be alarmed about.

Hurry. Kick the pebble. Hurry. Wait. She passed her Italian neighbor's place, with its chicken coop, then the bramble-covered vacant lot, the big rock at the corner sprayed with the words, *Fuck the dogs.* On she went, up the driveway. She did not realize yet how easy it would be to escape; that one day a solution would arrive, along with long legs, training, marathons: the secret being simply to keep moving, to outrun them. For now, all she could do was take hold of the front doorknob, push the door open, and then call out once.

Jane's mother fumbled with the bedroom door, then floated down the hallway. She planted a kiss on Jane's cheek with burning lips.

"How was your day?" The spark in Gretchen's eyes had been snuffed, and her hair was a static mess, as though brushing had confused her and she had stopped halfway through. And yet her half smile as she asked this question was sly. Yes, it was. Slyly gleeful at having escaped them. Like Miss Shapiro she had fled, leaving only this sepulchral, loose-haired, vodka imbibing presence.

"I'm calling Dad," Jane spat at her mother.

"No, don't. Please don't." Gretchen sat down heavily on the bottom stair and began to weep. Jane turned to stare at her. How could this happen? (And happen so often—each time taking Jane completely by surprise.) How could Gretchen—Gretchen the Lonely—Gretchen the Beautiful—turn into this weeping troll at the bottom of the stairs?

What made oblivion so worth it?

1968. Gretchen showered noisily, banging against the shower stall. Then she came upstairs in a clean floor-length caftan. She sat in her chair by the fireplace, hotly washed and scrubbed, as though for sacrifice.

At last Jane heard her father's MG rev up the driveway. His car door slammed, his key scratched the front door latch, his briefcase made a muffled thud on the parquet floor.

From her place in the kitchen, Jane could see both her father grimly mounting the stairs and her mother sitting with her ankles crossed, staring at the charred bits of log in the fireplace. Patrick came across the rug to stand in front of her. He shook his head, a jitter, almost a tic. Then he said: "Please Gretchen."

"I'm sorry," she whispered.

"No." He shook his head again, his face reddened, and he sat down on the hearth stone. Then, as though that were not far enough, he slid to his knees and placed his face in her lap. There was no sound, except for the refrigerator, which whirred and stilled, though the part in Patrick's hair had turned pink. Gretchen looked down from the vast field of her loneliness (she was crossing a moor at twilight, she was alone), and then she reached out and stroked the back of his head.

PETER KLINE
Universal Movers

We move the same packed box from house to house,
off the ancestral farm, now overgrown
with glorious, inedible rhododendrons
into the rented basement of a mud-lot
seeded for next spring. We sweat through shirts
to lug it six flights up to a Brooklyn flophouse
with a view of the subway station, ship it freight
to Porto, Tripoli, Piraeus, through
the Bosporus, points east, where one of us
will wait all day at customs just to claim it.
Rumors put us in a Baku teashop,
wrangling with the owner over the right
to commandeer his brother's pleasure boat
for the perilous night passage. How to convince
this gentleman? Our cargo is our right.
We fill out all the proper forms, insure
the contents (whatsoever they may be)
against flood, terrorism, sabotage,
human error, and the will of god.
We learn the local pleasantries, and buy
blindness from every overcurious eye.

Press it to your ear: only the rustle
of your own cheek against it. Pierce its side:
no fleck of velveteen, no globe of blood.
Too small for a printing press, or plough, or cello,
too heavy for a gun, or a lock of hair,

it makes us wonder. Still, we cannot raise
the courage or nostalgia to relieve us
of its mystery, and carry it like thieves
more ruthless for their inability
to find a buyer. We will not survive it.

PETER KLINE
Revisionary

for Kay Ryan

We sharpen our
lapidary eyes
toward flaws, and see
the easy cz disguise,
the phrase too pleased
to please. We loupe
the soldering for telltale
fracturing. We
will not be fooled.
But let us withdraw
the ball-peen hammer
from its velvet
swaddling, let us
address the listing
prong, the innocuous
ding: we stammer;
we miss the mark;
—with what great care
we overswing.

NICK LAIRD

The Mission

You are alone and walking down to Ryan's house and staring hard
at bags of rubbish thrown from cars on the old Dungannon road.
Overnight a revival tent has moored in the field as a rule reserved
for Fossett's Circus, or the cars of spectators for the *Cookstown 100*,
who picnic on the verge and cheer as packs of bikes pass by in blurs,
in Döppler roars, and dip at the corner like fins or sails and right again
and disappear. You don't know what you're looking for.

You are eight or twelve or seventeen, at home in the shortcut
through carpark and stockyard, the slit in the chain-link fence.
They put the plate glass windows of your father's office in
and you are with your mother, on the way to visit hers,
when you come to the soldier dead in the road, on his back
in a scatter of windshield glass and the shadow gone wrong
of blood gathering around him. You braked. You swerved.

When they take the town and shut the schools, you are turned
back at Morgan's Hill by men in Hallowe'en masks, weighing
rifles and baseball bats against their massed enormous guts.
As you try to get to class by Drum, you're turned away again
and warned. On Killycolp an autumn storm cowps the beech,
and afterwards they tell you how those cables in the branches
you just clambered through were electrified, and still live.

You are sitting in the house alone in the unlit living room
with your Uncle Jack's double-barreled split-piece shotgun
fed with scarlet cartridges and propped on cushions
to point at the hallway, as a brown panel van revs in the drive
and someone tries forcing the back door. You keep a list
entitled *Bastards* and when that spiral jotter's full, you get
another and print with care *New Bastards* on the cover.

You are dragging loads of turf in white or brightly
colored fertilizer bags from the outhouse to stack
by the coal bunker, and hear a human rumble coming
from the tent across the fields, as the midges dance
and tremor over concrete slabs and a muddy lawn.
You are watching now Ryan crying like a little baby
as he stumbles to the low stage to attest and get saved.

ANGELA PNEUMAN
Occupational Hazard

On a Friday, during his inspection of the sludge containment tank at the East Winder Municipal Wastewater Treatment Plant, Calvin's foot slipped off the catwalk—it was raining, the metal was wet—and his left work boot and left leg became submerged up to the knee in treated sewage.

"Whoops," said the plant manager beside him. The plant had a history of noncompliance, and the inspection had been unscheduled, causing the manager's big-cheeked Irish face to grow and stay red as Calvin lifted samples. Now the man visibly cheered up. "Occupational hazard," he said merrily.

"Shit," said Calvin. The sludge plastered his pants to his shin, oozed underneath the tongue of his boot. The manager showed him the hose, and he rinsed most of it off, but he knew the smell—sewage sweetened with chemicals—would inhabit the interior of his battered Taurus for days.

"Fragrant truffle," said Dave Lott back at the office, sniffing thoughtfully as Calvin passed his cube. "Hints of coriander."

"Right," said Calvin.

"Eau de *toilette*," Dave Lott said.

Calvin snorted.

It was past five-thirty, and the office—twelve beige cubicles at sea in the middle of a low-ceilinged room   was nearly empty. Calvin parked himself in his cube, which shared a wall with Dave Lott's, and glumly logged onto his computer. His shin and his foot felt clammy, but he was determined to ignore it for the fifteen minutes he needed to write up his report. Sometimes discomfort sharpened his brain, he'd noticed. On Calvin's other side, Robin, the sole female inspector, stood to put on her jacket, pulling an arm's length of thin, flat red hair out from the collar and letting it slap flatly against her back. It was so long that she probably hadn't cut it in twenty years, like the missionary women

Calvin had known in church as a kid. But he always liked watching her bring it up out of her jacket. It was long enough for her to sit on.

"Nuances of anise," Dave Lott said. "*An-us.* Get it?"

"Blow it up yours," Calvin said.

"Ah, poopy jokes," said Robin tiredly, on her way down the hall. "They never get old."

When she was gone, Dave Lott stood and peered at Calvin over the divider. He was a stout bald man with a gray thicket of a beard. The beard was an upside down triangle, shaped like pubic hair, Calvin had thought more than once. But you'd never say that kind of thing to Dave Lott's face. Calvin liked the guy, but carefully. He reminded Calvin of a cop, the way he could joke around and then get serious, all of a sudden, pulling rank and leaving you feeling like a jerk. Dave Lott's eyes were as gray as his beard, small and round, tiny gravel pits above gold-speckled half-glasses. The glasses were the magnifying kind you bought at the drugstore. The kind old ladies wore, which was another thing you'd never say to Dave Lott's face.

"Grab a beer?" Dave Lott said.

"Sorry, man. Got to get home."

Dave Lott nodded and pushed up the gold glasses, ambiguously, with his middle finger.

"Got to get out of these pants," Calvin said.

It was Thursday, and Calvin's wife, Jill, had her GRE class, and he had to watch the boys. Jill hated Dave Lott, though she wouldn't use the word hate. Everything was *dislike,* and now even the boys only *disliked* okra and *disliked* string beans, which sounded creepy to Calvin, coming from them—too much calm specificity. Jill disliked Dave Lott. She was friends with the man's first wife in the way he'd noticed women were friends, with the need to designate an opponent so they could know they were on the same side.

"Next time," Calvin tacked on, but Dave Lott just grinned through his beard and was gone. In a few days the man would be dead, picked off the periphery of Calvin's life, and Calvin would find himself trying to remember some significant detail about this, their last exchange; but in the moment there was only the dull noise of Dave Lott's work boots on the cloudy plastic hall runners tacked over the carpet, the suck of the steel door closing behind him, the trace smell of sewage coming from Calvin's own cube.

At home, Calvin's boys were in the basement watching their favorite video, a cartoon of *The Ten Commandments.* Jill stood in the bathroom before the mirror, gripping the cordless phone between her chin and shoulder while she did her eye makeup.

"I know it," she said into the phone. Her blue eyes flicked over Calvin as he popped his head in, and then she leaned into the mirror and blinked at herself. "I know it. No kidding." She was pretty, still— not like a movie star but like women on aspirin commercials, trim, sensibly brunette, smiling much of the time. She and Calvin were at war. Jill claimed to want another child, to want to try for a girl, and Calvin had found himself boycotting sex until they talked about it reasonably, which meant, he knew she knew, until he talked her out of it. He felt—unreasonably perhaps—that this desire of hers had nothing to do with him, though he couldn't prove that, of course, and couldn't imagine trying to explain why it mattered. Whenever he caught himself admiring her, it pissed him off. Now he wished he'd gone out for a drink with Dave Lott after all.

He headed to the kitchen, opened a bottle of beer and stared out at the backyard. A domed jungle gym rose from the grass like half a skeleton planet. Last year, Calvin had looked away for a moment to tend the grill and Trent, then five, had fallen the wrong way. When Calvin looked back, his son had crumpled quietly to the ground, staring at his broken wrist, more confused than in pain.

Now there was a shuffle on the linoleum behind him. Trent, in the doorway, raised his skinny arms and intoned, "Thou shalt not covet."

"Hey, bud," said Calvin, crossing the floor and passing a hand over the boy's fluffy brown hair.

"What's covet, again?"

"When you want something that's not yours."

"And then you steal it."

"No, I think it's just wanting it. They're separate commandments, aren't they?"

The boy nodded. "What's that smell?"

"Wastewater," Calvin said. He knelt by his son, palmed the boy's bony chest. Trent smelled a little too, kind of fruity, like he was due for a bath, but Calvin liked it.

"Can I sip your beer?"

"Nope."

"Can I hold it?"

Calvin handed him the bottle and took it back when Trent's lips fitted over the top, moving like a feeding fish.

"What did I say," said Calvin, standing. "Honor thy father and mother."

"Drinking's a sin," Trent challenged.

"Drinking's an *indulgence*. It's like sugar. It's fine if you don't overdo it."

"Sugar's a treat," Jill called from the hallway. "Drinking's a habit." Now she was standing in the doorway behind Trent, hands on her hips.

"Anything can be a habit," Calvin said.

"You'd know," Jill said.

"I'm sure that's supposed to mean something," Calvin said, "but you lost me."

Jack, their four-year-old, called Trent from the basement and the older boy backed out of the doorway and disappeared. At the counter, Jill began silently assembling her sandwich. Calvin watched the side of her face as she spread peanut butter carefully to the edges of one slice of bread, then matched up the top slice, crust to crust, as if it took great concentration.

Two nights ago, he overheard her tucking in the kids at bedtime. She told them that she loved them more than anything else in the world. "More than daddy?" Trent said, and Calvin found himself automatically curious about how she might answer, and then abruptly not curious at all. He moved quickly on past the door.

Jill looked up from the sandwich and narrowed her eyes. "What's that smell?"

Calvin extended his foot toward her. His pant leg was dry and stiff. "Occupational hazard."

Jill nodded grimly. She lifted a knife from the block, carved her apple into quarters, and zipped it into a baggie.

"Dave Lott got it worse than me," Calvin added, lying without knowing he was going to. "Up to the waist."

"Yeah, well, you know what I think about that," Jill said. "Couldn't happen to a nicer guy."

The horrible news about Dave Lott came on Saturday night, when the boys were in bed. Calvin was watching *Frontline* while Jill studied at the dining room table. "Listen to this stuff," she was saying. "Nine tracks, numbered 1–9, nine dogs, A–I. Dog A must always run in track 4. Dog G must always run beside Dog B, but never beside Dog C. Dog C always runs in track 8. Just to answer one question you have to make a chart, and it's a timed test."

The phone rang, and Calvin felt the mean satisfaction of answering it instead of responding to Jill.

"Calvin?" said a woman. For a second he couldn't place her voice, then realized it was Robin, from work. She'd never called him at home before. "Listen," she said.

He said, "Sure, hi Robin, go ahead," wanting Jill to hear how polite he was, what a good guy other people thought he was, the kind of guy people from work could call at home. And there was something about Robin's tone that made him consider the possibility of something sexual, some signals of a crush he'd missed. He felt tentatively flattered and compassionate. He anticipated telling Jill.

But then Robin kept talking, and Calvin was writing down the name of the hospital as if he needed the note to remember, as if both the boys hadn't been born there. Dave Lott was sick with an infection. A freak thing, one in a million. A fast-acting strain of strep invading his soft tissue, shutting down the circulation to his limbs, eating him into a coma.

Jill stood in front of the television as he told her, working her feet in and out of her slippers one at a time. "Oh God," she said. "From the sludge?"

Remembering his lie, Calvin had to shrug. "He had a paper cut," he said. It could have been true, for all he knew. "He and Dora thought it was the flu, at first." Dora was the second wife, and Jill rolled her eyes at the name.

"Well, I'm sorry," Jill said. "It's awful." She stretched her mouth into a flat, frank grimace that said she was sorry Dave Lott was in bad shape but that she wasn't going to change her opinion about him just because he was in the hospital, either.

Part of Calvin respected this—what he thought of as her bottom-line nature. But he disliked this about her too, and just now he wished he could think of something nasty to say, something to wipe the grimace right off her face. Inexplicably, he got a hard-on. He crossed his arms over his lap and leaned forward.

"Don't look at me like that," Jill said. "I said I was sorry."

Calvin had always appreciated bacteria, with all their invisible processes. He liked the intricacy of their names—fecal coliform, Escherichia coli, the whole hardy bacillus species. Bacteria were the secret to waste management, after all, allowing humans to live virtually on top of each other. They were nature's recyclers, breaking everything down to nutrients to be reabsorbed. It irritated Calvin the way people always acted like bacteria were the bad guys, and antibiotics were the good guys, because the antibiotics—their overuse, anyway—were what was screwing up the bacterial balance, tipping the scale toward the pathogenic. He'd shut down a few conversations with this rant. He'd refused to let the doctor prescribe antibiotics for his kids' sinusitis, insisting that their bodies would take care of it, and he had been right. Sure there were harmful bacteria—everywhere, in fact. If wastewater treatment plants were a bacterial smorgasbord, so was your basic kitchen counter. So was the surface of your skin. Like dormant cancer cells, you carried around any number of things that could kill you if you got cut in the right place, if your immune system were sufficiently worn down. You couldn't blame bacteria for killing Dave Lott, who was dead by Tuesday, before Calvin had even had a chance to stop by the hospital.

When the secretary sent out the mass voicemail, Calvin was the lone inspector in the office. He stood up and peered over the divider. There was Dave Lott's dirty coffee cup. There was the picture of his daughter from a few years ago, ten or eleven, her hair pulled tightly into two ponytails. The room's emptiness felt different, suddenly, and Calvin threw on his jacket and cleared out. *We weren't really friends,* he reminded himself. Even before he'd left off the occasional beer after work, that's all it had been—an occasional beer after work.

Outside, it was wet and chilly, with a substantial wind that whistled through some invisible gaps in the dash of his car. But the heater was enthusiastic, and even with the lingering sewage smell, he spent the afternoon driving two-lane roads he'd known his whole life. He turned on talk radio and didn't listen. It seemed stupid to Calvin, now, not to have had more beers after work with Dave Lott. It made him feel weak and pushed around by his wife, even though she'd never exactly told him not to. Now he imagined that Dave Lott had seen him this way, weak and pushed around. In his head, Calvin had an imaginary conversation with Jill, in which he told her in no uncertain terms that he would continue to have drinks with Dave Lott and any other friend— acquaintance—he saw fit. Then he imagined another conversation in which he told her something similar, but in a more reasonable voice. Perhaps Jill would have drawn it out into a lengthy battle. Perhaps she would have griped for a few days, then let it go. Perhaps she would have, eventually, admired his loyalty, even to a man she would forever dislike for leaving his wife, her friend.

He'd intended to surprise the Blue Ridge Treatment Plant with a brief inspection, but he found himself passing the facility and turning onto the back road that led to the small farm where he'd grown up. His folks still lived there, though they'd stopped farming and had sold off their acreage bit by bit, for income. Now, radiating from the scabby old clapboard farmhouse were five brick ranch homes for families who worked in town and wanted to build in the country. He didn't stop the car. Neither of Calvin's parents was sick, though his father had had a bout with prostate cancer. They were fine. A little shakier to get up from the table after Sunday dinner, maybe, but that was all. Now he slowed down to make sure their truck was in the driveway, and then he sped up, hoping they wouldn't see him pass if they happened to glance out the window.

Dave Lott's first wife, Pat, and their daughter, Jennifer, lived three hours away in Indiana. "Of course you'll stay with us," said Jill into the phone, and they arrived the night before the funeral.

Pat struggled to get each foot out of the car—she was a short, bulky woman—and stood up into Jill's arms. When they separated, Calvin saw that they were both dabbing at their eyes, though they'd had nothing good, between them, to say about Dave Lott when he was alive. Pat made a sound of perseverance—something like "whoo"—and smiled over at where Calvin stood three feet back on the grass. She reached for him, and he had no choice but to step in for a hug too. "Oh," she said, patting his back with both hands, pressing herself hard into his stomach. After what seemed like an acceptable amount of time, he pushed back from her, but she gripped his upper arms. "This really brings everything back up for me," she said. "This really peels the scab off the old wound." She smiled again, bravely. She had one of those mouths where a strip of pink gum showed above her upper teeth. It was the kind of thing you couldn't not notice, once you had. She held her smile and blinked at him, hard, until he felt compelled to smile back and nod as if he understood, as if they'd all been married to Dave Lott, as if he'd let them all down and now, on top of it all, he'd gone and died.

Through the open driver's-side door, Calvin saw Jennifer in the passenger seat, picking at her chin in the lighted visor mirror. When she got out of the car, she let Jill hug her, but the girl looked as if she felt more captured than embraced.

Inside, Jill offered the guest bedroom and the couch.

"We'll share the guest bedroom," said Pat.

"I'll take the couch," said Jennifer.

Pat gave Jill a prim, significant pucker, which Calvin watched Jennifer ignore. The girl had ragged, dark bangs that fell into her eyes, and the rest of her hair had been drawn into a braid that went down the back of her head and then another inch or two down her neck. There was a name for this kind of braid, Calvin thought. He set the bags in the living room, for the time being.

"I told Jennifer she could watch the boys while the adults talk," Pat said. "That would be fun for her. Take her mind off things." She passed a hand over the girl's forehead, brushing the long bangs out of her eyes. "Right, Jennifer?"

Jennifer's head reared back from the hand, slightly, like a snake.

"Whatever you want to do, sweetie," Jill said. "They're in the basement occupied with a video. You can lie down, or read, or just hang out with us. Who wants coffee?"

"Did you hear that, Jennifer?" Pat said.

Calvin wished the woman would give her daughter a moment's peace. She seemed unable to stop addressing the girl. And touching her too. Now Pat was squeezing Jennifer's shoulders, repeating, "whatever you feel like," as the girl hunched into herself unhappily.

"Are you awake?" Jill asked Calvin that night, entering their bedroom and turning on a low light. She and Pat had stayed up late, talking in the kitchen.

Calvin kept his eyes closed. He heard the zipper of her jeans, and the shushing as she pushed them down her legs. She moved, unnecessarily, to the table on his side of the bed, and rummaged in a drawer. He could smell her. Then she moved to the dresser and he knew she was slipping into one of the short nightgowns she'd taken to wearing to bed ever since she'd gone off the pill. It took two to have a baby, she'd said, and even though she couldn't force him, she'd informed him that she would no longer do her part to prevent anything.

"They're having such a hard time," Jill said. She turned off the light and got into bed. Under the covers, she pulled up the nightgown and pressed her bare breasts against his back. "Jennifer's in such a difficult stage," she said, moving her breasts against him. Her nipples grew hard, but just her intention, that she wanted something from him and was trying to get it her way, made her methods easier for him to ignore. "Dave wasn't much of a father to her, but he was all she had." She reached under the waistband of his shorts, from behind, moved her hand over his ass, and tried to work it between his legs. Calvin shifted away from her, slapping at her arm as if he were asleep.

"I know you're awake," said Jill as she rolled away. "You can't fool me."

At the funeral home, guests seemed to be dividing themselves up on either side of the aisle by who was friends with Pat, the first wife, and who was friends with Dora, the second wife. It was like a wedding, that way. Since Calvin would know everyone from work, he'd been enlisted to come early and stand toward the door at the back of the funeral parlor with the printed programs. He didn't mind this, as it kept him far from the half-open coffin. When Jill arrived with Pat and Jennifer, they all stood near him. Dora had taken her seat, already, left of the aisle in the front row.

"Will you speak to her?" Jill asked Pat.

"I don't know," Pat said, then, "don't look, honey," as Jennifer turned to find the woman. Pat pulled Jennifer close, and the girl kept her face blank. "I guess I'll have to say something." Pat turned to Calvin, as if for confirmation.

Calvin said, "Umm." What did the woman want from him?

Pat turned back to Jill. "I guess I should probably say something."

"Wait and see," Jill suggested, shooting Calvin a nasty look. "You shouldn't feel like you have to."

Visitors trickled in. Robin arrived with her husband, a thin man with an earring whom Calvin had met once before. They joined the small, stunned group of Calvin's coworkers who'd shown up early. Calvin had worked with these people for more than five years and had never seen them dressed up before. They'd all greeted Pat, then made their way to Dora, then stood at the far side of the room, inhabiting their clothes awkwardly, unsure of where to sit. Calvin had invited them all to the house, afterward, for a grim sort of reception. He imagined Dora would be receiving guests at her house too.

People who hadn't seen Jennifer in the years since she and Pat had moved admired, quietly, how she'd grown. Calvin watched the girl answer questions in monosyllables. When she spoke, her lips parted to reveal a chipped upper front tooth.

"You OK, honey?" Pat kept asking her between guests, keeping one square hand on the girl's back. "She hasn't said much since last week," said Pat to Jill. "Have you, honey."

"I've said stuff."

"Right," Pat said. "She's in that phase right now. You know, where everything I say is wrong?"

"I'm not in a phase," Jennifer said. "I just don't have anything to say."

"Last night you had something to say," said Pat. "That you hated me. Remember that?" To Jill, Pat said, "That's part of the phase too."

Jennifer rolled her eyes.

"It's hard to know what to say," Jill said. Which in itself was a great thing to say, Calvin thought, and if Jill had looked his way, he might have smiled at her.

"I know," said Pat. "I know. I just think we could give this phase a rest when something like this happens." She pushed the tips of her fingers up against her eyebrows until her eyes bugged out. When she let go, the loose arch of skin over each eye reshaped itself slowly. Calvin realized he was staring at this and looked away.

The door had been propped open with a rubber wedge. Outside, the sky was heavy and gray. It had been raining off and on all morning, and he could smell worms and wet pavement. He thought he could smell the storm drains too. There was a finger of cold in the air, as though winter hadn't given up. He watched a long blue car pull up and drop off a tiny elderly woman encased in a clear plastic rain shawl. She crept through the door with a walker and kissed Pat on the cheek.

"Oh, Miss Evelyn," Pat said. "Jennifer, this lady used to watch you when you were little."

"Do you remember me?" said the old woman.

Jennifer nodded and, in the first willing motion Calvin had seen her make, leaned down to hug the old woman. Over the woman's stooped shoulder Jennifer's face appeared suddenly nearer to Calvin's, eyes closed, nose shiny and broad. The skin on her lower jaw looked red and bumpy, and fine brown hairs were growing at the corners of her mouth, the kind Jill tweezed away in front of the bathroom mirror. As if she felt Calvin looking, Jennifer opened her eyes. They were small and gray, like her father's. Calvin felt for her. Her father dead, her mother hard to take, at best. Before the funeral, at the house, while standing before the closet, looking for one of his ties, he had heard Jennifer's shower through the wall. He heard the splash and patter against the stall, the rush of water hitting the tub, the squelching of plastic bottles of shampoo and conditioner. He was stepping into his pants when he heard something more, almost not a sound, it was so faint. He parted the hanging row of shirts and realized that through the thin plaster, he was listening to the girl cry. There was also a subdued smacking sound, as if she were bringing her hand hard against her forehead.

"Jennifer's a tough case," whispered Jill as they took their seats several rows back from the first. "Pat says she said nothing the whole drive down. Five hours. Pat thinks she's still in shock."

"I don't know about shock," Calvin said. "I mean, she can talk normally enough. Shock is a real condition. With real symptoms."

"I know what shock is," Jill said.

"Pat should give the kid a break. Some space."

"Space," Jill said, her breath an explosion in his ear. "You don't give a troubled kid too much space. Did you see that chipped tooth?" Jill glanced toward Pat and Jennifer in the front row to make sure she couldn't be heard. "Pat found her eating raw macaroni for a snack. Right out of the box. Hard as rocks. And this even before Dave died."

Calvin nodded at a man and woman they knew casually from church, who lowered themselves into chairs in the row in front of him. Jill smiled at them too, and grasped each of their hands. Then she turned back to Calvin and frowned. "Don't you think that's kind of strange?"

"Sure," Calvin said.

"Pat asked her why, and she said she liked the way it sounded in her ears. The crunching. She said she liked how sharp it was against her tongue."

"It's strange, but it doesn't seem like a huge thing."

"Pat worries," Jill said. "And now she has to deal with Dora on top of everything else. That's a hurt that's still fresh."

"She keeps it that way," Calvin said.

"What?"

"Nothing."

"I heard you," Jill hissed in his ear. "Pat didn't ask for any of this, you know."

"What?" said Calvin, as the organ picked up pace and volume.

"You can't even muster up the generosity to be nice. Don't think I don't see it."

"What?" said Calvin, touching his ear. He knew it was childish. "What? What?"

Jill shook her head and set her teeth.

The hymn was one Calvin recognized, "In the Sweet By-and-By," and its message was that everything would be OK after everyone was dead. In the front row, Pat's shoulders started to shake, and she reached for Jennifer's hands, clutching them to her chest. This pulled the girl's far arm awkwardly across her body, though she remained facing straight ahead, in the direction of the coffin. This and everything else seemed to Calvin to boil down to resistance—to giving in or not giving in, even when you couldn't say exactly what there was to be resisted or what made you want to.

After the funeral there was a confrontation in the parking lot. Calvin saw it coming. The second wife moving up behind Pat, Calvin's own nod to her, a woman he'd met only once, causing Pat to turn around on her heel. The second wife was already hugging Jennifer, and when the woman handed her a pocket-size book of collected love poems, explaining that they had belonged to Dave Lott's mother, Calvin saw the girl's chin trembling.

"How thoughtful," Pat said crisply, stepping in between them, extending her hand to the woman. "Thank you."

The second wife untangled her fingers from Pat's and passed a hand over her brown bobbed hair, as if it needed smoothing. "I loved him," she said, not very nicely.

"Fine," Pat said.

"I loved him," said the woman again. She turned to Jennifer. "You should know that."

Jennifer nodded. She looked nervously at her mother, who had begun to nod too.

"You loved him," Pat said, nodding, "and you want *my* daughter to know that."

"That's right," said the woman.

"Let's all take it easy," said Calvin.

"Pat," said Jill, "let's go."

"You loved him," Pat said again.

"You wouldn't know the first thing about that," the woman said.

"Don't tell *me*—" Pat started, but the second wife turned away. "He had a *family*," Pat called after her. "So don't tell *me*." The woman kept walking, and Pat began to shake. Calvin thought she might be about to collapse, which wouldn't help anyone. As he helped her to her rental car, her upper arm felt so soft and old that he found himself compelled to handle her tenderly. This made him cross.

"I'm sorry," Pat said to no one in particular.

"You were nice to even try to speak with her," said Jill. "Considering."

Jennifer stood to the side, trying to fit the book into her small blue purse. Pat sat heavily in the passenger seat but kept her feet on the pavement.

"Put your head between your knees," Jill said, and helped Pat flop forward.

When she raised herself, Calvin placed his hands on her stockinged calves and folded her legs into the car.

"I'm sorry," Pat said again. She clutched Calvin's forearm and closed her eyes, leaning her head back against the headrest.

"OK," Calvin said, his hand on the door. "We're all done here."

"I'll drive her," Jill said to Calvin, still angry and not looking at him.

"I'll go with you," Jennifer said to Calvin. It was the first thing she'd said to him, and her voice seemed light—too agreeable, like she anticipated being told she couldn't.

"Take Jennifer," Jill said, as if Jennifer hadn't suggested it. The girl was already moving toward Calvin's car.

Once they were on the road, it began to rain. The windshield clouded over and Calvin turned on the fan. Jennifer stared out the passenger window. She rolled it down several inches, moving her face toward the cool air. They drove in silence for a few blocks. Calvin was trying to decide whether it was a comfortable or uncomfortable silence. He wondered if it could be a different thing for each person or if perceptions about silence were mutual, like an odor in the room no one could ignore.

"I'm sorry about your dad," he said, finally. "I liked him."

Jennifer was still looking out the window. They passed a storage facility. Low, putty-colored buildings stretched back from the road for a good two acres. The thought of all that stuff, just sitting there, made Calvin feel heavy.

"You know how he died, right? Basically, he was eaten alive."

"He was very sick," Calvin said.

"I didn't think his job was even dangerous."

"No, no," Calvin said. "That's not it. It's not dangerous. This was just a freak thing. Hardly ever happens. He could have picked this up at the laundromat or in his own garage. Bacteria are everywhere. All kinds of bacteria."

"So then everywhere's dangerous," said the girl. She shrugged at the revised perspective, rolled down her window all the way and stuck her face fully into the air. Calvin wondered if she was going to throw up. He wondered if he should pull over. Her long bangs lifted straight off her forehead, standing vertically in the wind. He watched her observing herself in the passenger side mirror for a block. Then she jerked her head back into the car and let it fall against the headrest. Her lips moved, and she said something way in the back of her throat. "I hate her."

"Who?"

Jennifer smiled up at the roof of the car, exposing the chipped tooth. "I do hate her," she said. The girl's chest, with her two small beginning breasts, pulsed with what could have been laughing or crying, but she was still just smiling up at the ceiling. "What are we going to do when we get back to your house anyway," the girl said. "Just stand around?"

That was exactly what would happen. Calvin thought for a moment. "We could stop by the office, first, if you want. Your dad kept a picture of you on his desk."

The girl closed her eyes. It had been the right thing to suggest or the wrong thing, but it was out there now, and he headed in the direction of work. The rain was coming down hard, and the girl felt for the knob to roll up the window. Calvin adjusted the wipers to medium. Their motion and the rain outside made everything in the car seem more still. He turned off the defogger.

"My mother said that instead of telling her I hated her, I should have taken a dagger and stabbed her in the heart. She said I should have dissolved a bottle of sleeping pills into her coffee."

"Your mother's having a hard time."

"She's a drama queen," said Jennifer. "She's always having a hard time."

This sounded about right to Calvin, but it also seemed an inappropriate thing for him to confirm. He slowed for a light. The window had begun to fog again, and he switched on the blower.

"If it makes you feel any better," he said, "everyone hates their parents once in a while. I hated my parents. My kids are going to hate me, probably."

Jennifer looked at him balefully. Calvin felt old. And depressed. He remembered something he hadn't thought about in years. "What I used to do? I would pretend my parents had been in a car accident. Not that they were seriously hurt, or anything, just one of those fender benders. I'd be waiting at home, and maybe it would be raining out, like today, and I'd imagine that they slid off the road going really slow, and maybe hit a tree, or a fence. Just hard enough to bump their heads good. Not even any blood."

The girl was looking toward the window again, following the staggered water drops in their descending horizontal.

"Then I'd imagine them walking in the door, looking just like they always did. My father looks a little like Don Knots. But when they greeted me, it would be different, more polite, like they were talking to someone else's kid. My mother would ask me what grade I was in. My father would ask me who I liked for the Super Bowl that year. And I didn't mind telling them. Then I'd ask them if they had any kids, and they'd look at each other and smile and say no, they hadn't been blessed with children, and I'd know that the accident had taken me right out of their memory, and it felt great. I even kind of liked them."

"How old were you?"

"What?" Calvin said, pulling into his parking spot. "I don't know. Fifteen, maybe."

"I'm fifteen," she said.

The girl wore no coat, he realized halfway between the parking lot and the door. The rain was not heavy just now, but they had no umbrella, and by the time they reached the entrance, Jennifer's hair was damp, and the fuzzy wool of her dress showed rain spots.

Inside, in the green fluorescent light, the air was chilly. The office had emptied out for the funeral. It felt like coming in to work on a Sunday. Or like Calvin remembered feeling on the days he'd stayed home sick from school, as a child. Like he'd stepped right out of time.

Jennifer shivered, but shook her head when Calvin offered his coat. She trailed him down the plastic runner toward his cube. One quarter of a ceiling panel had grown soggy with rain, and water gathered into a drop and fell heavily to a puddle on the plastic. When Calvin's hard-soled dress shoes hit the spot, his feet slipped out from under him, and he slapped at the floor in a kind of undignified tap dance, grabbing the side of a cubicle to regain his balance. He looked back at Jennifer, but she was reading the name tags on each cubicle they passed.

Calvin tapped on Dave Lott's name tag when they reached it. "Want to sit here for a minute? Take some time?"

"OK," said the girl. She lowered herself into her father's desk chair. She opened one of his drawers and took out an enormous ball made of rubber bands. Then she put the ball back in the drawer and closed it.

"I'm just going to be right here," Calvin said, gesturing to his own cube, but the girl didn't look up. She was moving her hands along the top of Dave Lott's desk, picking things up and putting them back down.

Calvin went through some papers. He looked at the calendar on his computer and pulled files for the week's inspections. Then he saw that his voicemail light was on, so he listened to his messages. One was an announcement from the secretary about the funeral, closing the office for the day. Another message announced the reception at Calvin's house. When he hung up the phone, he stood and peered over the top of the cube to check on Jennifer, but she wasn't there.

He stepped out and looked down the aisle. Empty. He called, "Jennifer?" but the only sound was the dripping ceiling and the buzzing of the fluorescent lights.

At the other end of the hall, he knocked on the bathroom door, but it was empty. He stepped up onto Rex Hickman's chair, keeping a precarious balance over the wheels as he scanned the tops of all the cubes. Nothing. He called her name again, but the room gave off no resonance, the sound dead as soon as he closed his mouth, as if there had always been only the fluorescent hum of the lights and the rain worrying the flat roof. As if the girl had never been there.

He checked the secretary's office, next to the bathroom. Locked. He crossed to the other aisle, with its identical row of cubicles, and peered into each one, but they were all empty. As if everyone had died, not just Dave Lott, as if a bacteria had invaded the world and he was the only, lonely one with immunity. She wasn't in their supply closet, and she wasn't in the equipment room. He left the office and stepped out into the rain to check the car, but she wasn't there, either. Back in the office he checked every cubicle again. He called her name over and over. This time, when he poked his head back into the supply closet, he switched on the light and found her wedged between the wall and a stack of boxes filled with printer paper.

"What's the idea?" Calvin said. "I didn't know where you were."

Tears formed in the girl's eyes, and she wrapped her arms around her middle. The closet was on the outside wall, and it was chilly. The ceiling in here dripped, too, into a large plastic bucket that sat on an empty palette. The girl looked miserable and cold.

"Hey," Calvin said. "Forget it. It's no big deal." He reached for her shoulder and patted her awkwardly. When she didn't resist, he placed both hands on her shoulders and brought her close to him. The girl was shivering. She sobbed three times into his coat and then quieted, like she was forcing herself to stop. "It's OK," Calvin said. He moved his hand over her back and then let go, thinking of the handkerchief he kept in his suit coat pocket, a habit his father had instilled in him. But his overcoat was unbuttoned, and the girl reached her arms inside and around him, holding him at the waist. She pressed the side of her face very hard against his shirt. It was as if she were much younger, he thought, a child, or maybe much older. He moved his hand to the back of her hair, where his fingers found and followed the texture of the damp braid. The girl shivered against him, and he wrapped his raincoat around her with his arms. Against the roof, the rain came down steadily, like it was never going to stop. It rained 40 days and 40 nights, once, Calvin's grandfather used to say when conversation lagged. Calvin was thinking of using the line himself when the girl's legs parted on either side of his thigh. He thought it might have been an awkward accident, and he shifted, attempting to reposition her hips to the side of him. Beside his face the top box on a stack had gotten wet from another leak in the ceiling. As he tilted his head back to locate the leaky panel, the girl realigned her hips frontally against him. She began moving. First almost imperceptibly, then steadily, then with more and more urgency. It was a seeking need, intense and confused.

Calvin stepped backwards and felt another wall of boxes solid behind him. The girl stepped with him, into him, though he'd turned his lower body to the left, attempting to hold her and prevent her at the same time. She dropped her face to his chest again. He was only semi-erect, but she found this with the outside of one of her thin legs. He pushed her away and tried to look her in the eye, but her eyes seemed to go straight through to the back of her head. There was something vacant about her face too, like nothing you tried to do for her would make any difference. He rested his chin on top of her hair and kept her hips away from him, with his hands. She pushed her face against his shirt, rubbing it there like a cat and making wounded, wanting noises in the back of her throat. When he brought her body close, finally, it seemed like a kindness. It seemed like the only possible help. She went up and down on her tiptoes against him. After a time, still under the cover of his coat, he reached down to her knees, lifted her skirt, slipped his hand between her legs, and stroked her through her cotton panties to the rhythm of the rain until she shuddered, bleating, "I, I, I," into his shirt.

He held her for a moment more. Then he removed his coat and wrapped it around her shoulders. He tried not to think. He steered her, silently, back into the main room of the office, down the aisle of cubicles, and out the door to the parking lot. In the car, he turned on the heat. He started to speak, meaning to impress upon her how important it would be to say nothing. But the girl was blinking sleepily out the side window, the rain streaking subtle shadows across her face in the dying light, and he closed his mouth and did not disturb her.

The first guests had already arrived by the time Calvin pulled into the driveway.

"You ok?" he asked the girl before they got out of the car.

"Yeah." With the tip of her tongue, she touched the edge of her broken tooth.

Jill appeared at the door, and the memory of the storage room flipped off like a switch in his head. "Where have you been?" she asked, and when he told her, she nodded, and the tough set of her face dissolved. She was moved, and this moved him—his heart—toward her in an old way.

Jennifer entered the house ahead of him. When her mother rose, crying, from the couch to pull her close, the girl went stiff again.

"I'll get you some Kleenex," she said to her mother, and disappeared down the hall.

Calvin poured punch and made small talk with Robin and her hippie husband. When the nut bowls needed refilling, he did that. He said the same things about Dave Lott over and over. Nice things, about his sense of humor. And he shook his head with everyone else about the way he'd died. He did not picture the man in his head. The boys returned from the sitter's, and Trent stuck close to Calvin, closed-mouthed and shy around so many new adults. When Robin's husband tousled his hair, the boy drew back and leaned heavily against Calvin's legs, a neediness of the body that brought back the moments in the supply closet with the dread remembering of a bad dream. Calvin passed a hand over his own forehead. He felt Jill watching him from across the room, and when he met her tired eyes, she smiled. Calvin forced himself to smile back. He saw Jennifer approaching her mother on the couch.

"Hello," he heard her say. He thought by the way she said it—polite and kind—that she must be talking not to Pat but to the woman next to her. Then Jennifer said, formally, "I'm so sorry for your loss," and he realized she was talking to Pat after all.

Pat reached for Jennifer's hand, and the girl allowed it to be held. "Honey," Pat said.

"I'm Jennifer," she said, introducing herself to her own mother.

Pat blinked at her. Beside Calvin, Robin's husband was saying something, but Calvin wasn't listening. He watched Pat's face turn confused, with furrowed brow and pursed lips. Jennifer kept up her polite, sad, chip-toothed smile. She covered Pat's hand with her other hand.

Calvin turned back to the man next to him. From the corner of the room, he heard Pat cry out, "Jennifer, stop it."

"You all right there?" Robin's husband was saying to Calvin, whose stomach felt bad. Trent looked up at him, his dark eyes questioning.

"Go get ready for bed," Calvin heard himself say.

"Hey. Hey, Calvin," said the man. Calvin felt a strong hand on his shoulder.

"I'm OK," Calvin said. He brought his thumb and forefinger to the corners of his eyes. "I'm all right."

"You knew him pretty well, huh," said Robin's husband.

Across the room, Pat was saying, between great, ratcheting sobs, "I'm your mother." Calvin watched Jennifer, her face the picture of propriety, touch her mother's back as impersonally as a funeral employee. He thought he heard her say, "There, there." Pat dropped her face into her knees and covered her head, and Calvin lowered his eyes like every other guest in the room. He sensed, rather than saw, Jill hurrying over to help.

Calvin thought he might be sick. Then he took a deep breath and said to Robin, to her husband, "I need some air."

Outside, it was dark and cold, but the rain had stopped. Calvin sank down onto the back cement stoop. He reached behind him into the cinder block of the house's foundation where he and Jill always kept a fifth of vodka. For some reason it seemed different than keeping the hard stuff in the house.

When he'd told Jennifer about the thing he used to do with his parents, wishing amnesia on them, he hadn't told her everything. As a kid, when he kept up the fantasy of talking to his parents as if he didn't know them, something eventually reversed itself. The longer he imagined their benign responses, the more he felt uneasy instead of relieved. In his head, he'd become desperate, leading them down the hall to his room, showing them things that would prove they had a son and that the son was he. His underwear drawer, his private collection of colored chalk dust, meticulously stacked in film canisters along the floor of his closet. In his mind's eye, his parents kept nodding pleasantly, but without recognition, and this made the young Calvin suddenly, fitfully afraid. He began watching the clock, desperate for his parents to return. By the time they really did come home, he was so happy to see them that he found himself trailing them around the house, more helpful, suddenly, than was his teenage way, just to be near them, just to reassure himself that they knew him, until his mother said, one of these times, that he was behaving like a boy with a guilty conscience.

When Jill found him, sometime later, he was sprawled on the steps, staring up at the night. The sky had cleared in spots, showing stars and a very bright half moon.

"Oh, Calvin," Jill said, taking the half-empty bottle from him. She zipped up her coat and sat on the step above him. He leaned his head back on her knees, and she brushed his hair away from his forehead, like she did at night with the boys, like she had not done with him in a long time.

"Jill," he said, but his voice came out cracked and a little wild.

She shushed him. "Just be quiet," she said, still stroking his hair. Calvin thought he would cry from the feel of her hand. "This has been a day," she said. "Pat's a mess in there. Jennifer is a strange bird. She's saying she fell at the office. She's saying she hit her head and can't remember her own mother. She's way too old to pull this stuff."

Calvin took the bottle back from her and drank again. "I didn't see her fall," he said truthfully. "I didn't know she hit her head, but maybe she did."

"OK," said Jill. "Whatever. Only right now she's in there asking people if they've ever seen that nice woman who keeps crying. As if anyone really gets amnesia, Calvin." On his forehead, Jill's hand went still. Calvin closed his eyes. He thought if she would just ask him for something, anything, he could do it. He knew he would be willing, in this way, for a long time.

"Listen to me," he said, expelling all his breath with the words. Two ragged breaths later he tried again, but Jill moved her hand from his forehead to his mouth. "Help me," he said into her fingers. But the words were whispered, and she mistook them for a kiss, and smiled.

CLEOPATRA MATHIS
Dead Fox

We pretended to know nothing about it.
I withdrew to my childhood training: stay out
of swampy undergrowth, choked edges.
This was around the time
we were too cruel to kill the mice we caught,
leaving them in the Have-a-Heart trap
under the sun-burning bramble of rugosa.
But moving up the trail, we caught a glimpse
right at the start: the fox just over the hillock
on the dune-side slope, spoiling
the grass-inscribed sand. Neither of us looked—
it seemed best to back away.
On the dune's steep side
we surveyed what we'd come for: ocean's
snaking blue beyond the meadow, the silvered
blade-like wands lying down. Lovely enough
to hold ourselves to that view.
But the currents of an odor wafted in and out,
until the sweep of smell grew wider, wilder.
The heat compounded, and ugliness
settled its cloud over us, profound as human speech,
although by then we were not speaking.

MICHAEL MORSE
Void and Compensation (Facebook)

My friends who were and aren't dead
are coming back to say hello.

There's a wall that they write things on.
They have status updates. *What are you doing right now?*

For the most part, they seem successful.
They have children, which I can only imagine.

The hairy kid we called *Aper*, I haven't heard
from him and wonder if in every contact

there are apologies inherent
for feelings hurt and falling out of touch—

I'm sorry in the way that dogs out back
bark at the nothing they're trying to name.

Now the missing turn up online,
the immanent unheard becoming memory.

We have conversations that are flat
or we speak to one another in threads,

a wall more kind than faces posted downtown
when tower dust settled and sky went blue again.

When Leo died we couldn't believe he wasn't hiding,
that his laugh would not sound out, announce his return.

What a laugh. Goofy. His. Purely his
and out loud like a dog barking at stars.

Something heavenly. An application
against insults or things that spill.

That was Leo. And he left.
I don't think he meant to go

before he found some beloved and made
someone in and not of his image.

I want to find Leo on Facebook.
I want to discover that he's a chemist

and tell him it's like high school all over
with so much living, it was nice, to be done

and to see and hear from you after so long.
You seem great. You look exactly the same.

LYNNE TILLMAN
Tiny Struggles

He managed the walk to Main Street, three blocks, two long avenues, and didn't worry about how he looked—a big whitehead poking along the sidewalk. Things were getting better, not that Tiny knew the absolute right moment to leave his house, because out the back door his garden merged with theirs, and the neighbors might be around. Summer weekends, everyone hung out.

He could leave through the front door, but that resembled a first entrance in the middle of the second act, which was why, finally, Tiny quit acting. That excruciating second, when his presence on stage was unmistakably felt, disarmed him nightly. Even appearing in the Soaps got to him, but he'd made a bundle. Tiny's new existence in the country was awkward, remarkable—remarked upon by those who knew him—exciting, and maybe permanent. He'd figure it out as he went along.

"It's not really the country, the row houses on your block, they're city structures," one friend said.

"You're in the hood," another said. "The ghetto."

"It's a mixed nabe," Tiny said, imitating a nightly news guy. "The face of the real America."

Not much separated the houses, a few feet, low fences, honeysuckle, ugly weed trees no one bothered to dig up. To build high fences or plant overbearing trees could appear unneighborly or sinister. Inside his private domain, anything was possible, he could do anything, but he didn't, no one does, or few do, anyway. No one used all his freedom, and, wherever Tiny was, nameless others entered his mental space.

Upon awaking, Tiny pulled the curtains half-open, for some natural light and to show the neighbors he had nothing to hide. To his left, the neighbors were also city converts, professional people, architect and designer, a black and white couple, Nicholas and Arthur, who kept to themselves and had friends over occasionally. Tiny was invited when he first arrived, but informally they agreed to preserve a sense of the city and be neighbors who borrow a figurative cup of sugar.

Most days and nights, the street was dead quiet. A few shouts and bursts of loud music, nothing much. The other night, or early morning, was anomalous because Tiny woke up to cries and yowls that wolves make when their cubs are killed or kidnapped. An obese white woman, who sat on her ruined porch every warm day and night, was wailing to a disheveled, skinny man, You're not leaving are youYou'renot leaving me are youYou're not walking out are youYou're not you can't leave me. Tiny squirmed below the window ledge. No one had ever yowled at him, he found it kind of magnificent—the passion. Nothing like that, unless he counted the stinging e-mail rebukes from his older sister, Georgina.

Tiny, On the phone, you acted like everything was fine and dandy between us, and I'm supposed to pretend the way you do. You feel your behavior doesn't call for an apology. But when your friend's dog bit me on the calf, and their dog went RIGHT FOR ME, instead of comforting me, you said the bite was nothing, Look, you're not bleeding, you said. Nothing, no compassion. How would you like it if…

Family. Tiny couldn't escape them, even now, three hours away from them and their city. He was the baby and the tallest, perversely nicknamed Tiny. His given name was Theodore, after the fat Roosevelt, which his father thought was funny. His father had bought the farm six years ago, his mother was doing the big fade, and before he moved away, Tiny had split with his girlfriend of six years. His twin brothers were jerks, and his sister was angry at him for being born.

It was a new life he wanted.

Some stores in town were easier to enter than others. Some owners or managers welcomed him, some greasily, others held back, restraint or contempt, he couldn't judge. He was no judge; that was his father. This afternoon, the pale, lithe woman in the cheese store, her blond hair screwed into a furious top knot, seemed disagreeable. Tiny intuited that Top Knot despised selling jams and cage-free eggs from happy chickens. This is where I end up, she's thinking, slicing a chunk of aged Gouda for…She couldn't find words for him, Tiny decided—what and who was this tall, 40-something, pale-skinned, dark-haired man in faded jeans and an unironed shirt, untucked. He watched her, fascinated.

It was an up-and-coming town, at least it had been up-and-coming when he bought the house; now people were saying it would come back. The town will come back, you'll see, it always comes back. The town thrived and failed, an organism dependent on visitors who savored its Victorian houses and country-style stores selling thick bars of French soap and 1920s dish towels laundered in bleach. Now Tiny was moving through a fastidious space. He picked up a bath-size fluffy white towel, which could wrap a small car, and fingered its thick pile. He hovered over an ample bunch of dried lavender, whose scent offered instant sanity.

Mostly, the native population was out of work, blacks, whites, integrated and equally downhearted. The town kids' future didn't seem unknowable: taxes low, public schools abysmal. More and more stray cats, who would never be neutered, screamed in Tiny's garden because he liked cats and fed them scraps when no one was around. His sister always said, "You make your own messes." He couldn't walk on the grass without sliding in shit.

Main Street stretched on and on against real time. Tiny strolled toward an unhurried café or good bar; he wasn't hunting, exactly. The best bar in town served a mixed-up-everything clientele, and weekend nights drew a big crowd from surrounding towns smaller than his. His town. Our town. Above the bar's spotted mirror, to the left, Tiny read reassuring words on an old-fashioned blackboard. "Use PARA—word in sentence. Your sentence wins—Martini on the house!"

That Victorian she couldn't afford—paradise.

He advertised in the local paper for a paramour. His bad!

Tiny usually needed an incentive and took a seat at the long, white marble-topped bar. The only person he'd ever met, down one end, was a solitary, bookish man who dressed up as James Joyce, so Tiny forgot his name because he unfailingly thought, James Joyce.

Paradox, paralysis, parasite, parataxis, parallel.

Near Mr. Joyce, ignoring him, an exasperated fiftyish man exclaimed to his group, "It's not the fine arts, it's the construction business." Down the other end of the long bar, a svelte woman about his age peered at him. He drank his Vodka tonic. She peered again. Tiny smiled. She peered again, anxiously. He walked over to be friendly.

"Do we know each other," Tiny said.

"I'm sorry, I thought you were someone else. I'm not wearing my glasses."

"But I am someone else," Tiny said.

She looked perplexed, not amused, so he tipped his invisible hat and returned to his end of the bar.

Paradoxically, the fox…

He finished another Vodka, another sentence. "Who doesn't long to be a parasite and never work?" He handed the paper to the red-faced, buxom bartender. "No good deed goes unpunished, no bad deed goes unpublished," he murmured intimately, to restore his cool. This is a wit's end, he told himself.

Life's just full of niggling compromise. Tiny wouldn't sweat the small things; that was city life. Walking home along the dreamy back alley, Tiny fed his fantasies, starting one, replaying it, she's on her knees, starting another, staring at the huge blue sky, sun still a flaming red ball. The new version fails to start, he can't get it started, but how can he fail at his own fantasy. Defeated, momentarily, Tiny remembered his college friend Tom, who looked upset one morning in the cafeteria. Tom habitually dreamed he was flying. "Last night," Tom said, "I couldn't get lift-off."

His neighbors Nick and Arthur's lights were on, three more cars in their parking area meant guests, while his other next-door neighbors—renters not owners—sat at a long, wooden picnic table, eating corn and hot dogs. Barbecue smells, country life, the sweet life.

"Nice evening, folks, how're you doing?"

"Just great, how're you doing?" one of the men said.

Five adults and one child lived upstairs in the two-story house: two stringy white guys, one hefty black woman, one scrawny white one, all in their 30s; a lean, light-skinned black woman, 20 maybe, and a 10-year-old white boy. Tiny had heard the boy call both men "Daddy." He couldn't tell them apart, either. The family must view him as a weirdo. The weirdo in their midst. The scrawny white woman took her time responding, as if on delay. "We're fine, thank you…and how are you?" She had a singsong voice and emphasized "and how." He dubbed her the ironic one. The lean, young woman appeared to be sulking, her thin face drawn with cheekbones like flying buttresses. She didn't greet him at all, she scarcely raised her head, but he wished she had. Her name was Chelsea, her black cat, Satan. Unfixed, he was sure.

The old sun started its descent, and Tiny was aloft on his terrace, squinting at the newspaper and watching the birds on his lawn—sparrows—peck away at masses of birdseed he'd thrown into a super-large metal salad bowl. The birdseed company advertised its seed as irresistible to colorful birds—he'd had two Blue Jays, one redbreasted Robin. Hundreds of sparrows arrived the same time every morning and evening, positioned on the electric wires, a scene from *The Birds*, until he refilled the bowl. No one else fed the birds the way he did.

This was great, this was better than living in the country, he reckoned—it was sort of a city in the country, with benefits, like gardening, feeding birds and stray cats, renewal along with the seasons, the chance to be natural and free, because things were different here.

Tiny fixed himself another Vodka. Everyone spied on their neighbors, and why he cared about getting caught or being nosy, he didn't know, except it conformed with his being citified, a veneer to shed. Tonight, a large white-frosted cake appeared, ablaze with candles—the birthday of the scrawny woman, 35. The neighbors to their right, who kept a beautiful garden, were barbecuing in tandem; by outward appearances, they were white, one father, one mother, two sons, the traditional family. The hulking blond boys, close in age, 19 or 20, stood at the fence flirting with Chelsea. She leaned in, they leaned in, three bodies pressed against the flimsy barrier. He wondered which one she would choose. Not him, that was certain.

Tiny followed the progress of Chelsea's romance like a sitcom, a week of daytime backyard flirting and fence-leaning, the brothers in baggy shorts, she in her polka-dot bikini, then nighttime hanging out, until one evening Tiny spotted Chelsea in the other backyard, at their dinner table, while her family, eating their dinner, glanced at that other backyard, ruefully, and he thought, like a soothsayer, there's going to be trouble.

It didn't take long, Chelsea selected the bigger of the two. Tiny tried to gainsay why, because they both appeared to be good-natured hunks. Maybe one had a great personality or was a better kisser. Chelsea and the boyfriend pitched a tent for two in his family's backyard, and every night, they'd disappear, and every morning, she'd scoot back to her house, or, if she'd gone home to sleep, Tiny would awaken to the boy's calling her name, sort of mournfully, Chel-seeeee. She'd emerge from her house, sleep-deprived and sleepy-faced, and glowing. Chel-seeeee. Chelsea began saying Hello to him too. And then the boys did. She was blooming in her new world, from the looks of it a better one.

The two families didn't actually acknowledge each other. They weren't feuding but there was a gulf between them. Like families separated by the Berlin Wall, some in the East, some the West, unable to communicate, raised so differently. Satan regularly jumped over the fence into the wrong yard, and Chelsea carried him back, not saying a word, returning quickly to the other side. More and more, the scrawny woman turned her back to the girl, who was or wasn't her daughter, as Chelsea raced to that other backyard. And the scrawny woman started leaving garbage near Tiny's side of the fence, not taking it to the dump. When it started to stink real bad, he'd talk to her, gently.

The August weather lay heavily on everyone, oppressive as the country's news. Tiny couldn't eat dinner in front of the TV anymore, not at news time; and he couldn't avoid any of it, not by turning on the A/C or the TV. Things seeped in. Tiny and his one-way street were at peace, nothing grievous happening; the obese woman sat on her ruined porch like a Buddha, the skinny man coming and going, kids played in the street, and the guys next door became friendlier, by attrition if nothing else.

In October, the weather changed to bright and zesty, plants dying, trees bursting with fall. Tiny's days were OK, a little boring, or too good, so he knew it would change, because everything changed—better or worse, there was always change. "You can count on that," his mother used to say, before her dementia set in. Tiny would need to find work soon, but maybe he wouldn't be able to. He might fall in love, even with Top Knot. He might win the lottery, but if he won millions, so much he didn't know what to do with it, that would become a burden. Most lottery winners led rotten lives ever after, hounded by relatives, and some killed themselves. He would apologize to his sister, and promise her money when she needed it.

The weather turned colder, his first winter in the country.

He bundled into his old, heavy coat, swung his gray wool scarf around his neck, found a tote bag, and opened his front door to the world. He'd walk to Main Street, do his shopping, visit Top Knot, who had her moments. He didn't get far. Chelsea was standing in front of her house, her belongings on the street. Everything, all her clothes and CDs, had been flung out from the second floor. Five big, shapeless mounds. Chelsea, in only a T-shirt and jeans, was gathering up what she could, putting it in black garbage bags, and crying without making a sound. Tiny gathered stuff too and set it on the sidewalk. They did that together, silently, until her boyfriend showed up. He embraced Chelsea and looked at Tiny.

"They kicked her out," the boyfriend said.

"Kicked her out," Tiny said.

"Yeah, the shits kicked her out."

"Why? What happened?"

"Because she doesn't have a job. None of them got a job, but they kick her out, and she's just 18."

"She's jealous," Chelsea said. "She's jealous of me."

Tiny knew she was the scrawny blond.

"Chelsea's got nowhere to go," the boyfriend said.

"Nowhere to go," Tiny said.

The words sounded like stones.

The three stood together, Chelsea bending in toward her boyfriend for protection against the wind. They looked at him intently.

They wanted him to offer her a place to stay for a while, he had a house all to himself. He couldn't. It would turn bad. He just couldn't.

"Jesus," Tiny said, "this is really terrible."

"I don't know what I'm going to do," Chelsea said.

"She can't stay with us, me and my brother and her, and my parents," the boyfriend said. "It can't happen."

The wind whipped around them, and Tiny drew his scarf up near his mouth. He could pretend to be tone deaf or blind. He could explain that his mother was coming to live with him. But then it might happen. Stranger things than that happen.

"I'm sorry. I'm really sorry. I wish I could help you. You'll find someplace."

"Yeah," the boyfriend said, "social services or something."

"Something's gotta happen," Chelsea said.

"It always does. Something happens. You can count on things to change," Tiny said.

He could see their hope collapse. The three of them stood there, then the two of them looked at each other, maybe for strength, Tiny thought later. Chelsea faced him, purposefully.

"You one of those toxic bachelors," she said.

"Me? What do you mean?"

"You know, a fickle dude. A love 'em and leave 'em guy," she said.

"I'm not…

"You know, ambiguous," she said.

Ambivalent, she means, but he wasn't going there. "I just like living alone, that's all."

"Everyone has to live with themselves," the boyfriend said.

"Yeah," Chelsea said, "you have to live with yourself."

She said it fiercely. Tiny could protest more that he wasn't toxic, but it might be better to let her think he was ambiguous. Toxic Bachelor must be a reality show. He pulled his scarf tighter. It was freezing. She must be freezing, he thought. But she held her head higher.

"I can take care of your cat," he said.

It was a gesture.

"Satan?" Chelsea said.

"Sure, I can do that, if you want. I can take care of him for a while. If you want."

Chelsea studied him, her boyfriend studied him. They glanced at each other. It took a stupefyingly long time, and the ball was in her court. It was her call.

"No way, no fucking way," Chelsea said, fiercer now. "My cat goes with me."

She and her boyfriend bent down, grabbed some clothes, and carried the stuff toward the alley.

The way Tiny told it to close friends, he'd given her room, so she could reject him. He wouldn't ever know what she thought. Chelsea moved the next day. The scrawny woman's garbage stayed there, along with Chelsea's clothes, frozen, for a long time. Tiny heard rumors about where Chelsea lived and with whom, but the boyfriend didn't follow after her. That surprised him.

PAUL MULDOON
Whale Watching in Iceland

Scarcely had our break-of-day whale-watching trip on Faxafloi Bay
been canceled because of high waves
than our house-minding daughter would weigh
in with the news her dog, the selfsame stray
we took in fifteen years ago, has died. She insists on digging Toto's grave

hard by Oscar's, there on the crest of the leach field.
From almost three thousand miles away I emphasize the need
for the grave being sealed
with polythene. Even as I pondered how even-keeled
an eighteen-year-old may be, one track would bleed

into another where a deck boy's winched
down through a hole drilled
in the head of a sperm whale. Our daughter would no more flinch
from the pressure per square inch
than the deck boy who fills

his bucket with spermaceti. The gory-gorgeous trough
through which he'll toil,
pausing only to give a little nervous cough.
Whale watching in Iceland is something we'll now put off
till he returns with the last of the oil

from that massive skull
into which he's lowered himself, the massive oil-butt
over which a flock of fulmars and gulls
will continue to mull
till the tackle chain is hauled in and the ties are finally cut.

MARY O'MALLEY
From "Resident at Sea"

"Da molte stele mi vien questa luce"
　　　　　　　　　　　　　　　　—Dante

I. Sea Road, No Map

I said to you I will die if I stay
and you said Jesus we'll die anyway.
You spoke as if I did not exist.

What world would have me? A ship.
She moves me on from impossible Ireland,
the wrack of ties I have knotted
too tightly, things I do not understand
like gardens, sisters, why days
taste flat. We slide out the bay, past Salthill
leaving Galway rampant,
the drug dealers, the scrap merchants,

a city at the races, every horse wild eyed,
the merchant class handing one another rosettes,
flanks heaving at how well we are doing
under the lash. Under the last arch
three musketeers raise their cans
to another new hotel—how many new hotels
can the homeless need?
The buckfast kids under the bridge
will start no revolution,

the guns are moving in another direction
and gunmen have to make a living somehow.
Cliffs, birds, Blaskets slip by. I think
can we keep on going to Valparaiso
and never come back. Surely it will be easy
in Valparaiso, with oranges and tin hearts
and only one kind of fruit,
and no voice following
with one half of a conversation.

It was making day when I looked out
at the kind of beauty
that leaves death unthinkable,
purple slate, gannets rising in small explosions
and everything makes sense.
The world is round again and we are its sun
describing a horizon, ratskin waves stretch to America
lumps of sea rise under the bow and below
acres of drowned Ireland and a mountain.

The sea is streaming through him.
His eyes dissolving in salt water, sting.

Is this how the soul might know itself
fathoming, like two saints meeting

on the way from Rome,
one saying this is a flowering plain

picking a bluebell and offering his proof archly
the other saying this is the sea

and scooping up a salmon in reply
fathoming deeper intentions

small treacheries
the slant pitch of the deck

forcing the center inward
somewhere near the solar plexus?

Today, he'd be fined for the sea's bounty.

I am dissolving.
What would sing in me is the deep ocean

the roll and pitch of her voice
the wrecks, fish, instruments

the drowned and those who swim in her.
Land makes sense

from this distance, we hear
its jangled music like a score.

We shift destination to Nymph's Bank.
Dinophysis lures the scientists
now inland, now offshore
now, unexpectedly, to the sea floor.
Inside this small hub all is domestic
and office. Computers, phones, faxes
link us to land, to our houses
to the hand on the phone

(there is no hand on the phone)
in the hall, a kitchen in Donegal
a living room in Brest.
We wash our cups make snacks, watch
the progress of the deluge in England.

A young spaniel is swimming through the streets
and even this triumph of endless rain
results in comedy and grief.

The washing machine hums, someone coughs.
Helena is working out in the gym.
Miles away Ireland
is rich in tribunal and gridlock.

DON PATERSON
Burial

The body is at home in time and space
and loves things, how they come and go, and such
distances as it might cross or place
between the things it loves, and its own touch.
But for you, soul, whom the body bred in error
like some weird pearl, everything is wrong.
Space is stone, and time a breakneck terror
where you hold to nothing but your own small song.
No wonder you would rather stay asleep
than wake again to your live burial.
But sometimes, shrinking in your tiny keep
you make out through the thousand-mile-thick wall
the faint tapped code of one as trapped as you,
saying: *those high white mansions—I dream them too—*

SAM SULLIVAN
Lush Life

Sure, there was the giant knife, and the quick, fat slice
of cake in his right hand, but what always surprised me
was the night into which he stole. Hard and purring.
Luminous and thick. It seemed not a real place—
pines and bluffs and crashing waves as if it were
a symptom of his being, this world—all of it.
When was the last time we watched those last scenes?
Was it raining all of a sudden, so we had to run
and close all the windows in the house, and all that was left
to do was watch a movie? Was it after dinner?
Did I fall asleep, and wake to see my dreams
softly ebbing on the walls of the den? (a silent car chase,
and sex with somebody else, unlovely and roughly edited)
You were angry, I could tell; the silverware was rattling
in the sinkbasin. And you, James Dean, you kicked the old painting in,
the one of your great-uncle right there on the floor, tore
it right apart with a little pop! It must have surprised you
how easy it was to put your foot through—and still
it made my chandelier shake. The walls, my walls, weakening somehow,
slant inward in their perspective. They shoot a current
of hushed gossip along themselves, around and downward in a spiral,
across the molding and the plaster, down to the mossy rug at their base.
James Dean, how did you keep those dungarees up around your waist
without a belt, keep them from falling to the floor
of the planetarium in a blue puddle? Standing in your skivvies
and a white T-shirt, taking drags from your toothpick
and exhaling words. The liquid would reflect the little lights
in the domed ceiling, the night inside here damper
and darker by far than the one that awaits you outside.

RYAN VINE

Rule 2

I know what hills in the distance can do
to a boy: they can make him think

hills in the distance
for the rest of his life.

The best thing for you
would be to keep

your eyes closed
at all times, looking

for a way out.

CK WILLIAMS
Timeline

Count they teach me so I count I count to ten I count to a hundred a
thousand
then I'm taught math I add subtract multiply just as I'm told but they
never let on
I'd still now be obsessively trying to calculate how to make things
make sense

I've lived for instance as of today twenty-six thousand nine hundred
ten days
as long as Sidney and Burns put together Plath and Purcell Crane plus
Mozart
plus a few thousand sad for them but for me it all slides away into
the seethe

Eight years it took between grasping there was this mind-thing in my
head
and King's speech and the war when my conscience began throwing
its tantrums
and what have I managed to do with the five hundred and sixty months
since?

My life's a topological monster not enough room in the century I was
born in
too much in the one where I'll die so many blots and erasures maybe
I'll borrow
some other century to better graph my trajectory a good one say the
nineteenth

In twenty—let's see—six it would be to end at the end Jefferson dies
and Adams

the year before Blake then my crazily fortunate span later in nineteen
   aught zero
come Einstein's theory and Planck's Freud's *Dreams* cars and Kodak
   cameras

Between all in the length of my sprawl amazing Keats born and dead
   likewise
Van Gogh Whitman Nietzsche and Marx there's Gettysburg Wounded
   Knee
the futile revolutions this war that war and wait I've consumed a
   lifetime again

And here I am my own extinction in sight and everything still such
   a screw-up
all the old poverty and injustice plus our dear world so wounded
   "Give me a fear"
prayed Donne "of which I may not be afraid" but my fears square
   cube quadruple

If you could only cipher back to that day in first grade before
   numbers and start
over kindly Miss Watson commanding "Don't count on your fingers"
   but this time
though you cross your heart that you won't you do eight nine ten
   damn it you do

EWA HRYNIEWICZ-YARBROUGH
Objects of Affection

Each summer when I'm in Krakow, I make weekly trips to a flea market close to our apartment. This particular market also sells antiques, but it doesn't aspire to a loftier name, because it also peddles secondhand books, last year's issues of fashion magazines, handmade jewelry, items that aren't old in the sense that antiques are supposed to be. A valuable nineteenth-century chest of drawers or a gilded mirror enjoys good neighborly relations with an electric coffee grinder and rusty door handles. It would probably be easier to attempt a list of things that aren't sold there than the ones that are. If someone is looking for a rare item, his friends will invariably suggest going to the flea market. When I was looking for a desk, I first went there and bought a beautiful art nouveau table, which recovered its former looks after being renovated. I love the market because I love rummaging through old things and because I usually will find something that I absolutely want to have. I love running my fingers over the shapely back of a violin, tracing the grooves in a century-old high-back chair, or gently tapping a porcelain cup to hear it tinkle. I know that to some people viewing old objects with something akin to reverence is a silly affectation. But particularly there, in a country that wasn't spared violent entanglements with History, an old photograph, a water pitcher, a clock that stood on someone's mantelpiece and was miraculously salvaged from a bombed-out building—those mute witnesses to human life inspire awe and amazement at the mere fact of their survival. They connect us to the past and its messy materiality by making that past more concrete, more tangible. And in them we see the reflected wisdom of our simple human order.

I was a child of the fifties, growing up in a communist country beset by shortages of practically everything—food, clothes, furniture—and that circumstance may have been responsible for my complicated attitude toward objects. We had few toys or books, and we wore mostly hand-me-downs. A pair of mittens, a teddy bear, and a chocolate bar for Christmas were enough. Once in a while we also got skates, bikes, musical instruments. "Abundance" had no place in our vocabulary and in our world, but we were happy with what we had, in the way that only children can be. We were unaware that our lives were in any way circumscribed, although the reality we lived in trained us early on that there was a huge gap between wanting something and getting it. After all, even people with money had to hustle and resort to underhanded maneuvers, including bribery, to buy things.

For many years I had only one doll, which my father somehow managed to procure when I was four years old. Made in Germany, Gabriela had two long braids. She was a beautiful doll, not like the ones sold in toy stores, and although I had other dolls later, she remained special. When the mechanism responsible for her making a crying sound broke, we took her to the doll clinic. At that time nothing was thrown away if there was even a slight chance that it could be repaired. I had Gabriela until I turned fourteen when, in a grown-up gesture, I bequeathed her to my young cousin.

By the time I graduated from high school, I was a person of substance, or so I thought. The shortages never disappeared, but it was easier to get things. I had a Chinese fountain pen and two ballpoint pens, which I kept in my desk drawer and would only use at home. I boasted several records that my sister and I listened to on a gramophone player she had been given as a name-day present a few years before. Some of them were by the popular Polish rock bands, and one was Beethoven's Fifth Symphony, the only classical music record I had for a long time. I listened to it so often that to this day I can hum the whole piece from beginning to end. I also had a bookcase with a sliding glass front that was filled with books. My parents' books were arrayed on three broad shelves in the bottom part of a cupboard in what doubled as our living room and their bedroom. Although both my parents were readers, they rarely bought books, borrowing them instead from the public library. I was very possessive of the books I owned and only reluctantly loaned them to friends. When my younger sister took one out, I insisted she put it back in the exact same spot.

My possessiveness may have had a lot to do with how difficult books were to come by. They were published in small numbers, and there was such a huge demand for them among the intelligentsia that the good ones disappeared from stores very quickly. On my way back from school, I often made a detour and walked by the local bookstore to look in the window where new arrivals would be displayed. That was how I spotted a four-volume *War and Peace* that cost eighty zloty, not a negligible sum. I had only thirty. The clerk told me this was the only copy in the store. I knew the book would be sold soon, so I decided to go to my father's office and beg him for a loan, which he gave me at once. Clutching the money, I ran back to the bookstore, breathless and worried that the book would no longer be there. I realize that what I'm saying must seem pathetic to a person raised in the comforts of a free market economy where it's enough to think of something to find it immediately in the store.

It might sound more poignant if I said that books and records helped me escape the surrounding grayness and drabness and that my hunting for them wasn't solely motivated by my newly developed acquisitiveness or a collector's instinct. But if I said that, I'd be practicing revisionist history. The truth is that we didn't see the grayness and drabness—not yet. This realization came much later. So if it was aesthetic escapism, it was the universal kind, not fueled by our peculiar political circumstances.

My youthful materialism thrived in a country where materialism—unless of the Marxist variety—was unanimously condemned as the ugly outgrowth of western consumer societies. We knew this was just an ideological cover-up for the never-ending shortages. My brand of materialism didn't belong in a consumer society, either, because it was a kind of disproportionate attachment to things that was caused by scarcity, something unheard of in a market economy. I couldn't want more, new, or better. Such wanting was at best a futile and abstract exercise, so I learned to practice self-limitation. Paradoxically, however, I knew what I liked and wanted, and would have had no trouble making a choice had I been given the chance. When you're faced with overabundance, assaulted by things and more things, it's often difficult to say what you like or want, but that at least wasn't our problem. I don't mean to praise privation or claim that we were somehow better or more virtuous than people who inhabited a consumer heaven and whose wishes could be automatically fulfilled. I'm only saying that my relationship to things was developed under a different set of circumstances. I did care about possessions, no question about that. I wanted to hang on to what I had and now and then replenish my stock if I came across the right item. More often than not chance ruled my acquisitions. I had to sift through what was available in the hopes of finding something special among a slew of worthless objects. That was also true of buying the so-called practical items. I might have been walking by a shoe store when I spotted a delivery truck. That sight would have been enough to make me stand in line. If I was lucky, I might have ended up buying a pair of sneakers. I might have also wasted my time because I liked none of the shoes or couldn't get my size. People would often buy things they didn't need or want, just in case. You could never tell when those things might come in handy or be used to barter.

In the mid-eighties I came to America for an academic exchange program. That wasn't my first visit to a western country. In previous years, I'd spent some time in England and Germany and a semester in Florida at the invitation of a Fulbright professor who taught at my university. I saw stores overflowing with goods I didn't know existed. But in 1984, three years after brutal martial law that obliterated any hope for change, Poland experienced unprecedented shortages, as if the communist government was doing everything in its power to punish the recalcitrant populace. To buy meat we needed coupons, and the same was true of sugar. Chocolate was rationed too, but you had to have children to get it. Grocery stores had shelves stacked only with vinegar and low quality tea, called Popularna—Popular, the irony of whose name wasn't lost on us. Other necessities were so hard to get that serpentine lines formed in front of the stores before daylight.

A few days after I arrived in the United States, a friend took me to a supermarket on Long Island where she lived. I knew what to expect, but as I kept watching people piling item after item into their shopping carts until they looked like elaborate pyramids, I felt sick. Who needs so much food, I thought. This was almost obscene. Soon my own shopping habits changed and began to resemble the American ones—if not in quantity, then in the way I went about buying. But for many years I didn't quite shed my old ways. For one thing, I attempted to have all broken items repaired. I remember insisting that my husband take me to a repair shop to have a strap reattached to a sandal that I'd bought a month before. The sandals were cheap, I couldn't have paid more than $20 for them. To my dismay I discovered that fixing the shoe would have cost me more than half that price. I gradually learned the same was true of electronics and many other items of daily use.

My reluctance to part with something that could possibly be repaired, which, against my better judgment, I still exhibit, comes from my grandmother. I can also attribute to her my preference for well-made objects with a long life span ahead of them. I remember how she had often said that she couldn't afford poor quality. By today's standards she had few clothes, and she wore her coats, hats, and jackets for many long years. All her clothes were made to last, carefully sewn of good quality fabrics by a seamstress or a tailor. The same can be said about her shoes. She had only four pairs of them, a pair for each season, spring and fall counting as one, and one pair of "going out" shoes that she'd wear to name-day parties or family celebrations. She dutifully carried them to a shoe repair shop if any of them needed new soles, straps, or buckles. Her apartment was furnished in what I came to call utilitarian style: only the necessary items, simple, and functional, no bric-a-brac, no trinkets of any kind. The only older object in her place was an antique napkin holder, with a marble bottom and brass top whose origin I know nothing about. She must have developed this unsentimental attitude after everything she owned perished in the burning of her apartment building during the 1944 Warsaw Uprising.

After many days of hiding in the building's basement and the subsequent defeat of the Uprising, my grandmother was taken to a camp in Pruszkow with my aunt, who was barely a year old, and my mother, eleven at the time. My grandfather had disappeared at the beginning of the turmoil and found his wife and daughters much later. Grandmother had a baby carriage, a suitcase with a change of clothes, a handful of photos, and a silver sugar bowl that at the last minute she snatched off the table. I never thought to ask her about the sugar bowl, although I wondered why she took it. Besides the photos, that was the only item that had nothing to do with survival. I can see her hurriedly packing clothes, a mug, a spoon, maybe some cream of wheat for the baby. For a moment her eyes rest on the silver sugar bowl on the kitchen table, a wedding gift from her husband's aunt. She hesitates, then quickly wraps it in her daughter's blouse and puts it in the suitcase. Did she want to keep at least one thing from her apartment, as a reminder of the life she knew was about to end? Or did she just grab it thinking she might swap it for food or use it to bribe a German soldier?

Eventually, she ended up living for several months with a peasant family near Lowicz. They treated the survivors from Warsaw like their own kin, and Grandmother gave them the sugar bowl, the only thing she could give to repay their kindness. When Warsaw was freed by the Red Army, she went back, hoping that maybe her building was still there. She saw only its skeleton and her beloved city in ruins. Convinced that Warsaw would never be rebuilt, she decided then and there to move to the former East Prussia, now labeled the Recovered Territories. The family settled in a small town that was barely scathed by the war, with only a few ruins here and there. The majority of the apartment buildings and one-family houses were intact. Their former German owners fled in panic from the advancing Red Army. To save their lives they had to lose everything, abandon all the possessions they had accumulated over the years, just like Grandmother, who had to leave her apartment and all it contained. The difference, however, was that none of her possessions survived, while here the newly arrived, shipwrecked people moved into apartments that were furnished, had pots and pans, rugs, bedclothes, pictures, and all sorts of knick knacks.

I often wondered how my grandmother felt in a strange apartment where the smells of the previous owners still wafted in the air and the sheets were still warm from their bodies. Among strange furniture, salt shakers with the inscription *Salz,* faucets with Gothic script, she must have felt like an intruder. She missed her Warsaw apartment that she had patiently and lovingly decorated. Now she had nothing of her own, no objects imbued with memories, nothing to fill out the space and make it hers. She never felt comfortable surrounded by all these strange things, this post-German stuff as we came to call everything that had remained after the German exodus. She also sensed the wrongness of her situation, its moral illegality, even though it was done with official encouragement and approval. Contrary to the official propaganda, there was nothing she could recover in those "Recovered Territories."

When I was about ten, Grandmother, who, in the meantime, had divorced my grandfather, moved into her own small house on the outskirts of town. She took with her all the furniture that was in the apartment because that's what she had. She couldn't have just sold it and bought new items. To begin with, she didn't have the money, but even if she did, the rampant shortages of everything would have made buying new items difficult. She lived in that house for less than two years and hated the distance she had to walk to get to town. When she sold the house, this time she sold it with everything in it, and got a studio in a newly built apartment building that had the telltale look of communist-style residential architecture. She was relieved to get rid of all the post-German objects she'd never considered hers. Because her new place was tiny, she needed only a few items to furnish it. Those post-German items were more attractive and better made than what she had bought, but at last she had things that belonged to her. And once she furnished her place, she never replaced anything in it, and she lived to be ninety-three. Her furniture and all her other possessions were functional and practical, and that was all she cared about.

My grandmother passed away in the fall of 2001. My mother was no longer alive, so the task of dismantling Grandmother's apartment fell to my aunt. I told her I'd like to get something that belonged to my grandmother, a keepsake. My aunt was at a loss because Grandmother had none of the items that family members usually keep after a person's death. I ended up with a round glass paperweight and some photos. My aunt took the napkin holder and my sister a metal basket where Grandmother kept needles, receipts, and small change. Was the paperweight an object that was full of memories for me? Not really. I knew that it was hers and that it was in her apartment, but it wasn't like those things that overwhelm us with nostalgia when we hold them or look at them. I have a lot of memories attached to Grandmother's apartment, the many times I visited her, the meals she cooked for me in her cramped kitchen, and I know that these memories are more important than a trinket I could have inherited. But sometimes I do wish she had left behind some things she valued and loved, which I could keep now and later pass on to my daughters. My grandmother is still alive in my memories. My daughters' memories are limited, as we could visit her only in the summer. When I'm gone, she will die a second death. An object that belonged to her could then serve as a reminder of her life, a souvenir connecting the different generations.

When I came to America, I left behind everything I owned in Poland. I arrived with a large backpack and a suitcase the size of a carry-on, which contained my clothes and a few books. In this sense my situation was like my grandmother's, but there the resemblance ends. My circumstances weren't the result of a war or a historical upheaval. Yes, I did lose things I was attached to, but they didn't just disappear. They simply changed owners, and most of them remained in the family. And unlike my grandmother, I felt I needed things for my emotional well being. My future husband had a lot of books and records, all of which I happily adopted as mine. Gradually, we filled our house with more books and records, more photos and photo albums, china, pictures, artwork, Christmas decorations. Some years later our daughters' dolls, teddy bears, drawings, seashells, rocks, homework, and school projects were added to the trove of important objects. I'm not a hoarder, but I'm sentimental about things.

My attachment to objects was put to a test the year of our cross-country move, from California to Massachusetts, where we live now. We knew we had to get rid of a lot of stuff. I decided to pack most of our belongings myself, separating the items of value from the ones relegated to the giveaway pile. The process was lengthy, and it exasperated my husband who has a very down to earth, no nonsense attitude toward possessions. He urged me to throw things away, since most of what I wanted to save I would never use or even look at. But with many objects I felt as if I had opened a sluice gate: I was flooded by memories. And once that happened, I knew I had to keep those items, no matter how trifling they would seem to someone else. I kept my daughters' newborn caps, their christening gowns, their first diaries with lockets, the cards they wrote to me on Mother's Day. I kept some folk art pictures, vases, plates, table runners I got from different relatives in Poland, even though I knew they would stay in the attic until the next inventory. And against my husband's advice to toss them, I even salvaged some items that he had as a child, like two model tractors he received at five from the Delta Implement Company in Indianola, Mississippi, and that now adorn the top of the bookshelf in his study. Will our daughters hang on to these things when the time comes to dismantle our house? I have no way of knowing. I do suspect, though, that they will want to keep our collection of books with its many first editions, the artwork, the photo albums, my mother's and my jewelry, a few antiques we have, and the Polish stoneware that I've been collecting for years. Maybe they will even keep some of the things that my husband wanted condemned to the junk pile. Maybe they'll be grateful to things for the delight they give us and the lessons they teach about the triumph and defeat of mortal matter.

Some years ago, in a world literature class, I was teaching Tadeusz Borowski's *This Way for the Gas, Ladies and Gentlemen.* One story in the collection, "The Man with the Package," a mere four pages long, provoked a very lively exchange. The story's main character is a Jew who has the position of a Schreiber in Birkenau's hospital—a position that for a long time offers him protection other prisoners don't have. Besides clerical work, his duties involve accompanying Jews selected for the gas chamber to the wash room, from which they are taken to the crematoria. One day the Schreiber himself comes down with the flu and is selected for the gas. On his way there he carries a cardboard box tied with a string; the box contains a pair of boots, a spoon, a knife, and a few other items. Seeing this, the story's narrator says: "He could show a little more good sense...He knows perfectly well...that within an hour or two he will go to the gas chamber, naked without his shirt, and without his package. What an extraordinary attachment to the last bit of property!" Just like the narrator, my students found the Schreiber's behavior bizarre. They couldn't understand why, when faced with imminent death, he would hang on to what were to them worthless things. They hadn't yet learned that objects help us exorcise some of our fears, that they are stronger than we are, perfect and independent, that they give us a semblance of permanence and grant a stay against chaos, darkness, oblivion.

A Profile by Stacey D'Erasmo

Colm Tóibín is a gentleman. A very witty, charming, lively, and sometimes deliciously louche gentleman, but a gentleman all the same, though one senses that he might not wish for that to be said too loudly. He has the beauty of a boxer—strong chest, light on his feet, precise in his movements and in his dress, and with a large, expressive face, gentle eyes. He keeps his elbows in. When I first met him a few years ago, I was surprised at how much he laughed, how graceful he was in conversation, how good he clearly was at putting others at ease. He's one of those people who are experts at getting you to talk about yourself and come away feeling that you've had a fascinating exchange. I was surprised because his work is so exquisitely built, so melancholy, so subtle and so spare. I might have expected a wallflower; he is anything but that. He has a great eye for style, knows his way around Yohji Yamamoto. At the same time, something is held in reserve. There is a zone of privacy around him that is less specifically personal than it is existential, ontological. "My influences," he says, "are Hemingway and Henry James"—two writers who couldn't seem more different stylistically and as men, but who share, in their work and in their lives, a core of silence, of a great deal left unsaid. That silence is resonant, abundant, like a room just after the orchestra has stopped playing. It is anything but empty.

Born in Enniscorthy, County Wexford, Ireland, in 1955, the grandson of a member of the IRA and participant in the 1916 Enniscorthy uprising, son of a teacher and a part-time office worker, he says succinctly that his ambition when he was young was "to get away from them all." Get away he did, first to University College Dublin and then farther afield, living in Barcelona from 1975 to 1978, where he taught English. He went back to Ireland and worked as a journalist, travel writer, and editor in the '80s, venturing to Africa and South America; in 1987, he published *Bad Blood: A Walk Along the Irish Border*, a nonfiction account of walking the tense border of Ireland in the summer after the Anglo-Irish Agreement. The fiction writer in him emerged slowly. He can't recall any mentors, but, he says, "My mother had written and published poetry before she married, and my father's brother, who died in his twenties, had also written poetry. When I was twelve, I began writing poetry. I started writing fiction about twenty-four, twenty-five." His father also died when he was twelve, a conjunction of loss and art-making that he has noted, somewhat reluctantly, in interviews. In fact, he adds to his primary influences of Hemingway and James, "the death of my father" along with "going to Spain; my homosexuality." He published his first novel, *The South*, the story of an Irish woman who leaves Ireland for Spain in the '50s to become an artist, in 1990, when he was thirty-five. Publication didn't come easily. "My poems," he recalls, "were no good and no one would publish them. My short stories were no good and no one would publish them. My first novel was good, but everyone turned it down. Then a small publisher in London did it."

From there, however, Tóibín rapidly came into his own. *The South* was shortlisted for the Whitbread First Novel Award. It was followed in 1992 by *The Heather Blazing*, winner of the Encore Award; *The Story of the Night*, 1996, winner of the Ferro-Grumley Prize; *The Blackwater Lightship*, 1999, shortlisted for the IMPAC Dublin Prize and the Booker Prize; *The Master*, 2004, winner of the IMPAC, the Prix du Meilleur Livre, the Los Angeles Times Book Prize, and shortlisted for the Booker; and *Brooklyn*, 2009, winner of the Costa Novel of the Year. Along the way, he also published the short story collection *Mothers and Sons*, 2006; *The Modern Library: the 200 Best Novels Since 1950* (with Carmen Callil), 1999; the biography *Lady Gregory's Toothbrush*, 2002; *Love in a Dark Time: Gay Lives from Wilde to Almodovar*, 2002; and edited *The Penguin Book of Irish Fiction*, 2001. His two most recent works are the collection of stories *The Empty Family*, 2011; and a collection of essays on Henry James, *All a Novelist Needs*, 2010. He crisscrossed the Atlantic—twice the Stein Visiting Writer at Stanford University; visiting writer at the Michener Center in Austin, Texas; currently the Leonard Milberg Lecturer in Irish Letters at Princeton University. He contributes regularly to the *New York Review of Books* and the *London Review of Books*. In 2004, he curated an exhibit at the Chester Beatty Library in Dublin entirely composed of blue objects from their collection. He lectures, reads, and travels widely.

However, for all the impressive and wide-ranging cosmopolitanism of Tóibín's career, four of his six novels take place in or near Enniscorthy. Some begin there, some end there, some take place entirely there. Hearts and minds in struggle with themselves is a frequent theme of Tóibín's, perhaps most gorgeously realized in his novel *The Master*, which concerns the unfathomable loneliness of Henry James, but which also threads through the roiled psyches of the ambitious, flinty woman artist of *The South*; the conscientious but isolated middle-aged judge of *The Heather Blazing*; and the semi-closeted, British gay man living in Argentina during the time of the generals in *The Story of the Night*; among others. Mind moves on mind, broods, goes to war with itself, connects, or, with devastating self-consciousness, fails to connect. The loneliness of the main character is always far larger than any name one might wish to put to it. Identity, national or sexual or even as an artist, is never quite the whole point. Something unsaid always remains, giving shadow and dimension, a counterlife, to his quiet, terse, crystalline sentences. If one were to score his novels, one might use Satie or Philip Glass. The world rages, visibly and pungently, in his work, but his heroes and heroines are always walking near the edge of the crowd, looking at the sky or the sea, holding what love they get close. Tóibín himself has built a house that overlooks the sea in County Wexford, not far from where he grew up. He speaks of it with pleasure and pride. "When I'm away," he has said, "it fills my dreams."

The most recent time I saw Colm was at a crowded book party he was throwing for another writer in New York. The room was full of wonderful, exceptionally smart people. It was spring; he was circulating with aplomb, pouring wine, laughing, welcoming, flirting, creating an atmosphere of delight. The crowd got bigger, and the night went on for some time. It was terrifically fun, and yet I couldn't help but feel that its intensity was also due to the complexity and depth of the mind of our host, who wrote, in the catalog for the exhibition of blue objects, "The imagination at work is always alone, no matter how strong a tradition or sense of community. The mind making images does so singly, in moments of fierce concentration, suddenly, as though this had never been done before, as though the task of now were the only task there ever would be." It was that, as well, that he brought to the party, and we were all somehow glad of it, though perhaps we wouldn't have credited an innate solitude, or a house in Ireland by the sea, for our worldly pleasure. —*Stacey D'Erasmo is the author of the novels* Tea, A Seahorse Year, *and* The Sky Below. *She is an assistant professor of writing at Columbia University.*

A Plan B Essay by Thomas Mallon

Voyager 2 traveled another 800,000 miles today.

Launched on August 20, 1977, the spacecraft is still sending data to the radio telescopes of the Deep Space Network in the Mojave desert around Goldstone. Any information dispatched today—about the solar winds that Voyager is flying through—will have taken thirteen hours to travel back 8.6 billion miles from the solar system's outer reaches. I'm writing this at 8:00 P.M. in the east, which means that the Sun must be getting ready to set upon the radio dishes. Soon enough it will be time for whatever astronomer is still in charge of Voyager 2 to hit the Save button, or tear off the day's printout, and call it a night here on Earth.

Observatories near Canberra and Madrid will take over as the world turns through its next dozen or so hours, but perhaps someone has to stay behind at Goldstone and keep watch on a few beeps and oscillations and blinking green lights. I think, at this increasingly late point in my life, that I wouldn't mind being that person, the one who keeps faith in the wee hours with this fantastical, faraway old contraption. Since I was twenty-five years old, Voyager 2 has been taking the species, in the gentlest and least imperial way, toward the rest of the cosmos. To put things in something like Neil Armstrong's famous terms—it carries no man, but it carries mankind.

Voyager 2 was launched five years after Apollo 17, the last mission to take human beings beyond Earth orbit. And yet, Voyager 2 has probably carried with it more of human personality and culture, more of the species' story, than any of the manned spacecraft that went to the moon. The "golden record" aboard it contains pictures, as well as sounds—birdsong, Bach, Chuck Berry—designed to entice some unknown group of interstellar beings into snatching the craft and giving a listen. The ship's primary work, long since completed, was to fly by and photograph the planets of our own solar system. It encountered Jupiter in 1979, Saturn in '81, Uranus in '86, and Neptune in '89. While passing by the latter, it noticed geysers spraying out of a moon called Triton. (Yes, there's a Voyager 1, actually launched two weeks *after* its twin and also still on the road, but it never got to see Uranus or Neptune and thus lost the chance of being my favorite of the two ships.)

Voyager 2 will eventually pass within a mere twenty-five trillion miles of Sirius, the sky's brightest star, though we'll never know it, since this not-especially-close encounter won't occur for another 296,000 years. But the craft should continue transmitting signals, speaking to us, until maybe 2025, the year I'll turn seventy-four. I now realize that, if I'd chosen to, I could have spent my whole adult life and career in support of its journey: hitting the Save button; tearing off the printout; being a good and faithful servant on the lowest rung of the project's organizational chart. I'd now be about three-quarters of the way through an alternate life akin to that lived by a hauler of bricks up the Pyramids: one of anonymous but worthy labor in the service of something eternally important.

I would have no desire for promotion, and no prospect of it. I was never an exceptional student of science, let alone math. My difficult, yearlong experience of trigonometry, the only subject in which I ever earned a C, left me convinced that it was a kind of hoax, like a set of phony cave paintings. But my feelings for astronomy, formed during the days of Project Mercury, have always had an authentic, if still half-educated, fervor. The actual heavens have been a substitute for the religion from which I walked away, a stellar instead of sacramental route to revelation, smoother than the earthbound ten-commanded one I might have kept slogging along.

I hero-worshipped astronauts but had no desire to be one; I have never even learned to drive a car. And yet I have always had the sense that a piece of me was on the machines we sent through, and now beyond, the solar system. The current position of Voyager 2—trackable on the screen of my computer, the digital numbers changing by the second—is real to me: I can almost see and feel it moving, can tell you that since I started handwriting this sentence in my low-tech way, the spacecraft has silently roared another 1,400 miles through the darkness.

As preoccupations go, this one of mine may seem oddly "futuristic" for a writer who has usually been so focused on the past. Not one of my seven novels has been set in the present, let alone the future. Even *Aurora 7*, my book involving Scott Carpenter's Project Mercury space flight, looked back twenty-five years in an attempt to reconstruct American life in 1962. The literary criticism I've written has more often than not taken me into belletristic realms where the subject matter—old letters, forgotten diaries—is gathering plain old dust, not stardust. So how does all this far-out cosmic rumination fit in? How does it not contradict everything else?

The answer seems clear to me. The farther out you go in space, the further back in time you're traveling. Think of how long it takes light to reach us: in the daytime, our cheeks are being warmed by sunshine that spent eight minutes getting here. On February 24, 1987, the astronomer Ian Shelton, at an observatory in Chile, saw with his own eyes a star explode in the heavens—witnessing it the way one might a street-corner shooting. But he was looking at something that had happened 170,000 years ago. It had taken that long for the explosion's light to traverse the billion billion miles to the Las Campanas Observatory. The stars we live under are not the promise of some future; they're the literal light of the past. Our journey toward them goes in reverse, not forward.

Voyager 2's journey may eventually bring it to one of the "exoplanets"—bodies orbiting stars the same way Earth orbits the Sun—that astronomers began discovering only in 1992, fifteen years after the spacecraft's launch. These exoplanets are now being detected by the dozen (they probably number in the billions), and some of them may well be temperate enough to support the sort of life that would be recognizable to us. And maybe creatures on one of these spherical specks will eventually snatch Voyager 2 and extract its golden record, its letter from our world.

I won't of course be here for that—any more than I expect still to be alive when humans set foot on Mars, something I once believed would happen before the year 2000. But I do hope to be here in 2025, when its signal at last gives out and Voyager 2 starts on its lonely way, untethered by communications with home, like a sailboat disappearing over the horizon. On the day that happens, when I'm seventy-four and Scott Carpenter is an even 100, perhaps I'll remember to whisper

"Go," the word he long ago heard in his earphones, after his rocket rose from the launch pad.

Thomas Mallon's eight books of fiction include Henry and Clara, Band-box, Fellow Travelers, *and the forthcoming* Watergate: A Novel. *His nonfiction appears in* The New Yorker, The Atlantic Monthly, The New York Times Book Review, *and other publications. He currently directs the Creative Writing program at The George Washington University in Washington, D.C.*

From the Archive: An Interview with Seamus Heaney

Reprinted from Issue 18 of Ploughshares, Fall 1979.
(guest-edited by James Randall)

Seamus Heaney has been at Harvard University teaching two writing courses during the Spring semester. The interview took place in Cambridge, Massachusetts at Michael Mazur's studio with James Randall and Seamus Heaney seated on a couch, tape recorder between them, and Michael Mazur working on sketches of Heaney for a monotype to be used for the cover.

Randall: I'd like to start with a political question. Is it possible for a poet to live in Belfast now?

Heaney: Of course it's possible for a poet to live in Belfast still, if he chooses to do so. Longley has made a very definite choice to live there, so has Paul Muldoon, Frank Ormsby and a number of younger poets. But those three I mention are at a stage of self-consciousness where they are doing it as an act of choice. I think their motivations for staying on would vary. I left in 1972 not really out of any rejection of Belfast but because... Well, I had written three books, had published two, and one was due to come out. I had the name for being a poet but I was also discovering myself being interviewed as, more or less, a spokesman for the Catholic minority during this early stage of the troubles. I found the whole question of what was the status of art within my own life and the question of what is an artist to do in a political situation very urgent matters. I found that my life, most of my time, was being spent in classrooms, with friends, at various social events, and I didn't feel that my work was sufficiently the center of my life, so I decided I would resign; and I now realize that my age was the age that is probably crucial

Cover Monotype: "Seamus Heaney" by Michael Mazur,
originally appeared on the Fall 1979 cover of Ploughshares.

in everybody's life—around thirty-three. I was going through a sort of rite of passage, I suppose. I wanted to resign, I wanted to leave Belfast because I wanted to step out of the rhythms I had established; I wanted to be alone with myself.

JR: Did you feel a sense of guilt about leaving?

SH: Well, I suppose the violence and the crisis in the public domain and the demand that was made on every writer heightened and made more urgent a lot of questions I had been thinking of for myself. I ended up in Wicklow partly through chance because Ann Saddlemeyer owned a cottage there and she'd heard from someone that I was thinking about moving. We had actually thought about moving into County Derry—still in Northern Ireland—but we were certainly going to leave Belfast. Then Ann sent us a letter saying she had this cottage in County Wicklow and would we like to rent it. Undoubtedly I was aware of a political dimension to the move south of the border, and it was viewed, I think, with regret by some, and with a sense of almost betrayal by others. That was because a situation like that in the north of Ireland generates a great energy and group loyalty, and it generates a defensiveness about its own verities. Some people felt rejected by my leaving, but it wasn't a matter to me of rejecting anyone but of my own growth. The crossing of the border had a political edge to it because we were opting to go into the Republic. But I was quite content in a way to accept and undergo that political dimension because I had never considered myself British. If I'd gone to London, there wouldn't have been a murmur about it—at least among my Ulster contemporaries. I had no doubt about the rightness of the move itself but I was bothered by some of its consequences, such as seeming to break ranks with my friends there.

JR: Who are the Protestants and who are the Catholics in this group?

SH: Longley is Protestant and so is Derek Mahon—but Derek was never entangled with the Belfast faithful, as it were. I always think of Derek as the Stephen Dedalus of Belfast, the man who is an ironist and who refuses to serve that in which he no longer believes, whether that covers family, church, regional loyalty or whatever. I feel uneasy talking in these terms—Catholic and Protestant—but I suppose it's worth it. Muldoon and Ormsby are Catholics. James Simmons lives in Coleraine and is also part of the Ulster twilight, as I sometimes call it, and he's a Protestant. In the 1960s there' was for a while, I think, a sense of discovery and exhilaration among my generation that we were moving an inch or two past the old pieties, and rigidities, and the old divisions. It was a liberal as opposed to any kind of radical political action, a coming together. But it wasn't advanced on the kind of banter and suspicion of the earlier generations. The older generation in Belfast made jokes with each other about priests and ministers and eating fish on Friday. It was all a kind of backslapping, hearty, uneasy, jovial, but they never really approached each other intimately or really approached the matter of what was wrong in the society. I think that we felt that we were carrying things a little further than that in our own lives to start with and that we would maybe eventually find some way of behaving that would be exemplary for everybody.

JR: Was it the Trouble that caused this sudden flourishing of poets in Belfast?

SH: I don't know. I don't think it's a positive fact like that. I met Longley and Mahon in 1962-64, and that's four or five years before things started. I think it was as simple as this: we were a first draft of young writers, Derek, James Simmons, Michael Longley and myself. We had books published one, two, three, four in about four years. Suddenly for young aspiring bright writers about the university and province there were published poets, speaking their own idiom, their own dialect. Young writers could see that a book was something that the man walking around the same streets had made up; it wasn't something awesome and different, or impossible. So I think there was a direct effect, almost a sociological effect, on their confidence in their own abilities. Paul Muldoon and Frank Ormsby were students of mine at the University and although I'm not saying that my class was a big influence on them as poets I think they got some self-confidence in seeing a member of their own community on the University staff and publishing books. There was almost a literary professionalism about for the first time, and the Troubles were contemporary with it. There is a connection at a deep level perhaps between the public demons and the private demons that were possessing people. The writers registered that connection but everybody in the place felt it within themselves.

JR: How do you feel about Yeats, about his aristocratic attitudes, about his poetry and its dangers for young poets?

SH: Well, the poetry is a magnificent brave gesture, brave in the heroism of the posture and finally braver still in accepting the defeat of that heroism. He was great as a craftsman, as a rhetorician, as a man of enormous creative energy not only within his own work but in the organizational things he did—like inspiring Synge to take a central role in the Abbey movement. George Moore, even though he scoffs at him, finally respects him enormously. I think Moore says somewhere that the Irish Literary revival sprang from Yeats and returned to him. I have nothing but respect for the purity of motive in his life and the enormous effort and amount of work that was done by him. Yeats's hack work of the 1880s and the '90s is awesome, the amount of work he did on fairy tales, on Celtic literature, on propaganda for Irish literature, on internal politicking on controversial local literary matters—that ambition to create an audience. This is all cliché ridden, about creating an audience, but when you see the actual committee work he did, the articles, and so on—I have enormous respect for him for that.

JR: And what about the posture of the man and the poems?

SH: He was always talking about the rancorousness of public life in Dublin and about opinion and how it makes a stone of the heart, and this is true to a large extent. But he also had the prejudices of his caste. He was against O'Connell for his rancorous mind but O'Connell, for God's sake, gathered the whole historical Irish Catholic nation together. Yeats's Catholic figures are interesting. For instance, there's Red Hanrahan, the devil-may-care poet, the beggars, the fishermen, and there's Paidín. Now Paidín stands for all that was trying to discover itself in 19th century Ireland; that is, the Irish Catholic middle-class was trying to move out of the penal laws of the 18th century toward all the rights that go with a republic in the 20th century—which was a hell of an advance on 150 years of living in the hedges. Now, Yeats's vision of culture was pure and patrician and all that, but it was peremptory and arrogant—it disdained history to a large extent. It disallowed middle-class life and set its face against all things commercial and self-consciously modern. Read "The Municipal Gallery Revisited" and that last advice "Irish poets, learn your trade!" The Irish Literary revival was powerful and it did create a myth that is still operative in people's minds: the dignity of the nation of Ireland and the dignity of Irish literature. And these people creating the myth were mostly from the Protestant caste. They went about it within their own lights, and fair enough.

JR: One of the early books that Yeats edited was a collection of Carleton stories.

SH: That's right. But you can contrast Carleton to Yeats; what Carleton hears when he puts his ear to the soil of Ireland and its underworld, he hears this rosary of almost exhaustion and patience, very different from whatever Yeats and Synge and Lady Gregory hear. When Synge goes to Aran in the late 19th century he hears the keening, almost a pagan cry, and Synge takes this wild, heroic pagan outcry against the universe and takes that as the spirit of Ireland and describes it in *The Aran Islands*, the wildness, the brutality and so on. That was perhaps a mystification. The real thing was much more deprived and defeated. And you have to go from Carleton to Kavanagh in rural Ireland before you get the authentic thing picked up.

JR: It is picked up in Kavanagh?

SH: Yes, I think so. It's interesting to link Kavanagh's *Great Hunger* with Carleton and with Brian Merriman's poem "The Midnight Court" in Irish. Brian Merriman's poem is a much more delightful work of art, more energetic, much more sexually and spiritually liberated than

Kavanagh's. You see in Merriman what was lost in the 19th century. Then Joyce puts in everything again. Joyce takes Paidín for his subject. Yvor Winters, a very wrong-headed kind of critic in many ways, said that if you read Yeats you'd think that Ireland was a country dominated by country houses, populated by beggarmen, and people riding horseback. You'd never think that if you read Joyce.

JR: It is true I think that Yeats's poetry and vision was dominating other poets for a long time.

SH: Yes. You see that in a poet like F.R. Higgins, a man who was once described as writing "a kind of crepuscular Leinster pastoral." He's a nice poet, but Kavanagh did a devastating article on Higgins, talking about the way the word "gallivanting" appears throughout his works. He used that as a stick to beat him with. There was too much fake Irishry in Higgins for Kavanagh, and Yeats was indeed responsible for that.

JR: You feel now that Yeats isn't dangerous as a figure to modern Irish poets, in the way that Milton was, say, to 18th century poets?

SH: I don't think so. No, I think that he's an enormous help in this way: he shows that by dint of fierce commitment to the art you can pay into the public life. And yet Yeats wasn't as beyond rancor or beyond politics as he pretended to be. Denis Donoghue very rightly points out that Yeats always disdains opinion and disdains politics and says "we have no gifts to set a statesman right" but that's an English statesman he's talking about. He was never afraid to set Irish people right. So, I think Yeats's example as a man who held to a single vision is tremendously ennobling—he kept the elements of his imagery and his own western landscape, the mythological images, and he used those and Coole Park, he used those as a way of coping with contemporary reality. I think that what he learned there was that you deal with public crisis not by accepting the terms of the public's crisis, but by making your own imagery and your own terrain take the color of it, take the impressions of it. Yeats also instructs you that you have to be enormously intelligent to handle it.

JR: In terms of—to move away from that slightly—but in terms of Philip Hobsbaum, the Englishman who taught in Belfast, what did he mean to you, bringing in the Edward Thomas kind of thing, basically an English kind of approach?

SH: I would say that I began to write, first of all, before I met Hobsbaum; my sense of literature was necessarily a sense of English literature. I had very little sense of Yeats, at all, only some of his early stuff. The poetry that meant most to me was Hopkins. It was only when I started to teach Yeats after about 1966 that I began to think about him and it was not really until 1970-75 that I confronted him in any way. And as far as my, so to speak style is concerned, as far as my ear was educated, it wasn't educated by Yeats, it was educated by certainly by Hopkins, Keats...

JR: Who else directly influenced you?

SH: When I was at college and later at university it was poetry with a thrilling physical texture I loved. I remember the first time I read John Webster's plays responding to them with enormous pleasure, and there is in Webster that very dark brooding violence in the imagery, very physical, scalding, foul images. I took great pleasure from that. When I started to teach them in 1962, I remember getting Kavanagh's work for the first time. I was now twenty-three years of age. And I read *The Great Hunger*, that was a thrill to me. Suddenly my own background was appearing in a book I was reading. And then I remember the day I opened Ted Hughes's *Lupercal* in the Belfast Public Library. And that was again a poem called "View of a Pig" and in my childhood we'd killed pigs on the farm, and I'd seen pigs shaved, hung up, and so on. So again, suddenly, the matter of contemporary poetry was the material of my own life. I had had some notion that modern poetry was far beyond the likes of me—there was Eliot and so on—so I got this thrill out of trusting my own background, and I started about a year later, I think. I had some poems here and there, in the *Irish Times, Belfast Telegraph*, and *Kilkenny Magazine*—a poem called "Mid-Term Break—and Philip Hobsbaum was in university. I forget how we got in touch, but anyhow he started the group. Longley wasn't in that to start with—I didn't know Longley at this time at all—he was either in Dublin or had just come up from Trinity College in Dublin. The same with Derek Mahon. Sooner or later I urged Hobsbaum to get Longley to come along—about a year or a half-year later. And we met, I remember, in Hobsbaum's class. Derek only went once or twice, but I saw Derek with Michael often. We met in Longley's flat quite a bit, just casually. Three young poets, and Edna [Longley] and Marie [Heaney]. Yet Philip Hobsbaum was really the one who gave me the trust in what I was doing and he urged me to send poems out—and it's easy to forget how callow and unknowing you are about these things in the beginning. From a literary point of view, Derek and Michael were more sophisticated about what to do. They had read Louis MacNeice, they had met MacNeice, and they had met other poets. I had never met anybody. They had more a sense of controversy with Hobsbaum and Hobsbaum didn't go for their work because he thought it was too elegant. He was a strong believer in the bleeding hunk of experience. So there was an edginess therefore, and I was favored and they weren't.

JR: Actually, they were maybe at an even more developed state. Was he sort of particularly interested in more metrical stanzaic rhyme?

SH: No, he didn't have any particular rhyme bent—he was quite happy with poetry that thumped along in iambics or in open forms. But there was, I suppose, in the air at that time—since I was reading mostly contemporary British poetry just then, Norman McCaig from Scotland, Ted Hughes, R.S. Thomas, and then the general atmosphere just of magazines and so on—there was a tail-end of the so-called "Movement," and the metrical thing was there. But, of course, my sense of poetry was drawn from my reading in university: conventional English literature. My ear was kind of baked from the beginning into the iambic pace. And it was also inclined to, as I was saying, the kind of sprung rhythms and the knottier textured kind of writing. We all, in some ways, took our first note from that neat-ish, late fifties-early sixties British writing, but I don't think Hobsbaum consciously fostered that—unconsciously, maybe. I never had the slightest doctrinal problem about meter or non-meter. In fact, one of the things I think about and used to worry about was an American hang-up about meter.

JR: How did you see that?

SH: Oh, you know, that meter was dead and so forth. As Thom Gunn says, meter is an abstraction until it is embodied in a poem, and there are successful poems in meter and there are unsuccessful ones in meter. I think one of the greatest collections of poems in the last fifty years was Lowell's *Near the Ocean*. Which is a kind of triumph of meter, of intelligence, and of morality.

JR: But Lowell has gone both ways. And what about you yourself?

SH: Well, I wrote a fairly constricted freeish kind of verse in *Wintering Out* and *North* in general, and then in the new book *Field Work*, I very deliberately set out to lengthen the line again because the narrow line was becoming habit. The shortness of a line constricts, in a sense, the breadth of your movement. Of course, a formal decision is never strictly formal, I mean it's to do with some impulsive thing, some instinctive sense of the pitch you want to make. And with *North* and *Wintering Out* I was burrowing inwards, and those thin small quatrain poems, they're kind of drills or augers for turning in and they are narrow and long and deep. Well, after those poems I wanted to turn out, to go out, and I wanted to pitch the voice out; it was at once formal but also emotional, a return to an opener voice and to a more—I don't want to say public—but a more social voice. And the rhythmic contract of meter and iambic pentameter and long line implies audience. Maybe I've overstated that.

JR: What I want to ask you along that line is, I think there is more commitment in your poetry, a social commitment.

SH: Yes. Certainly *Wintering Out* and *North* were attempts to go on from a personal, rural childhood poetry, attempts to reach out and go forward from a private domain and make wider connections, public connections. But I didn't want to start plying the pros and cons of the Ulster situation in an editorializing kind of way. I had no gift for that anyway, and while I did have a fair hoard of resentment against the Unionist crowd, I still felt hesitant about hammering a sectarian job, declaring UDI for the Catholic/Gaelic sensibility. That would only have ratified the sectarian categories which had us where we were. I wanted to find a way of registering refusal and resentment and obstinacy against the "Ulster is British" mentality, but at the same time I wanted my obstinacy to leave the door open for repentant Unionists. But apart from the politics of the thing, I was incapable, artistically, of breaking with my first ground and my first images. So *Wintering Out* tries to insinuate itself into the roots of the political myths by feeling along the lines of language itself. It draws inspiration from etymology, vocabulary, even intonations—and these are all active signals of loyalties, Irish or British, Catholic or Protestant, in the north of Ireland, and they are things that I had an instinctive feel for, as a writer and as a native of the place. So you have those language and place-names in *Wintering Out*, like "Broagh" and "Anahorish" and, in its own way, "The Other Side." And I think those poems politicize the terrain and the imagery of the first two books. And I think when you get to "The Tollund Man" in *Wintering Out*, you can see a similar development of the possibilities of "Bogland" which was the last poem in *Door Into the Dark*. There was a definite attempt to widen the scope of the thing. But you know, I want to pull back from all that because I have begun to feel a danger in that responsible, adjudicating stance towards communal experience. I just feel an early warning system telling me to get back inside my own head.

JR: And what about this bog-people idea, is that communal?

SH: Well, I've gone over this ground so often by now I'm a bit self-conscious about it. You see, the bog was a genuine obsession. It was an illiterate pleasure that I took in the landscape. The smell of turf-smoke, for example, has a terrific nostalgic effect on me. It has to do with the script that's written into your senses from the minute you begin to breathe. Now for me, "bogland" is an important word in that script and the first poem I ever wrote that seemed to me to have elements of the symbolic about it was "Bogland." It was the first one that opened out for me, that seemed to keep going once the words stopped, not really like the other poems that were usually pulled tight at the end with little drawstrings in the last line or two.

JR: Often with a moral?

SH: Yes, clicking shut like little boxes. Then this poem came drifting past me and instead of putting it behind me, I followed it, and it led me to P.V. Glob's archaeological study of peat-bog burials in Iron Age Jutland. A marvelous book called *The Bog People*, full of photographs of these victims, men and women who died violently and were ritually inhumed in the peat. One of those finds in particular has had an enormous effect on anybody who ever looked at it, the head of a man called now The Tollund Man. The Tollund Man seemed to me like an ancestor almost, one of my old uncles, one of those moustached archaic faces you used to meet all over the Irish countryside. I just felt very close to this. And the sacrificial element, the territorial religious element, the whole mythological field surrounding these images was very potent. So I tried, not explicitly, to make a connection between the sacrificial, ritual, religious element in the violence of contemporary Ireland and this terrible sacrificial religious thing in *The Bog People*. This wasn't thought out. It began with a genuinely magnetic, almost entranced, relationship with those heads. I wrote "The Tollund Man" and it was an extremely important poem for me to write because the first line of it said, "Someday I will go to Aarhus / to see this peat-brown head." And when I wrote that poem I had a sense of crossing a line really, that my whole being was involved in the sense of—the root sense—of religion, being bonded to something, being bound to do something. I felt it a vow; I felt my whole being caught in this. And that was a moment of commitment not in the political sense but in the deeper sense of your life, committing yourself to something. I think that brought me a new possibility of seriousness in the poetic enterprise.

JR: This came mainly through *The Bog People*?

SH: That was a growth period, all I'm saying is that. I'm very angry with a couple of snotty remarks by people who don't know what they are talking about and speak as if the bog images were picked up for convenience instead of being, as I'm trying to take this opportunity to say, a deeply felt part of my own life, a revelation to me. Then I went to Denmark—this whole period of my life was one of richness and at the same time of unease.

JR: But the experience of going to Denmark fulfilled what you hoped it would?

SH: Yes, it fulfilled it within my life, and the rest is a matter of the poems, isn't it? I've perhaps talked too much around and behind the poems here.

JR: It does seem an area that poets often would rather not discuss.

SH: Yes, but it's six or seven years ago now. I don't like, as Paddy Kavanagh says, "viewing my soul from the outside." But when it's become a ring on the tree maybe you can inspect it more easily.

JR: You were looking for some kind of metaphorical release, and you found it very satisfactory?

SH: Yes, and that was 1969. The year 1970-71 I spent in Berkeley and that was also a releasing thing. I didn't meet or become friends with the West Coast poets, but I became very conscious of the poetry of Gary Snyder. I saw Snyder; and Bly was living in Bolinas that year. He read a couple of times around the Bay Area. The whole atmosphere in Berkeley was politicized and minorities like the Chicanos and Blacks were demanding their say. There was a strong sense of contemporary American poetry in the West with Robert Duncan and Bly and Gary Snyder rejecting the intellectual, ironical, sociological idiom of poetry and going for the mythological. I mean everyone wanted to be a Red Indian, basically. And that meshed with my own concerns for I could see a close connection between the political and cultural assertions being made at that time by the minority in the north of Ireland and the protests and consciousness-raising that were going on in the Bay Area. And the poets were a part of this and also, pre-eminently, part of the protest against the Vietnam war. So that was probably the most important influence I came under in Berkeley, that awareness that poetry was a force, almost a mode of power, certainly a mode of resistance. Then the second thing was this mythological approach that Snyder and Bly were advancing: as far as I was concerned, their whole doctrine was too programmatic, but it suggested new ways of handling parts of my own experience. And then the third thing was a release I got just by reading American poetry, in particular coming to grips with Carlos Williams. In the poems of *Wintering Out*, in the little quatrain shapes, there are signs of that loosening, the California spirit, a more relaxed movement to the verse. It isn't as tightly strung across its metrical shape. The first poem I wrote when I came to California is the last poem in the book, a strange poem about weightlessness and drifting. This was just after the first moon shots.

JR: What direction do you think you are moving in now?

SH: I remember writing a letter to Brian Friel [Irish play-wright] just after *North* was published, saying I no longer wanted a door into the dark—I want a door into the light. And I suppose as a natural corollary or antithesis to the surrender, to surrendering one's imagination to something as embracing as myth or landscape, I really wanted to come back to be able to use the first person singular to mean *me* and my lifetime.

JR: And what kind of subject are you taking up?

SH: There are basically three blocks in the book. The poems are much more open, I think. I called it *Field Work* chiefly because I couldn't find another title. I think the poems in the book are quietly pitched. But I hope they aren't slack. There are a group at the beginning which are semi-public poems, elegies, meditations. Three of them, for example, are elegies for people who were shot, one of them a second cousin of my own who was shot arbitrarily. He was a carpenter in Armagh and he wasn't involved in anything at all political but was just coming home from a football match in Dublin. Then a man named Sean Armstrong whom I knew at Queens and who had gone to Sausalito where he became part of the commune-pot smoking generation—he came back to Belfast in the early seventies to get involved in social work and worked at children's playgrounds. And he was shot by some unknown youth. And the third elegy of that type was for a man I knew very well called Louis O'Neill, who used to come to my father-in-law's public house in County Tyrone; he was blown up on the Wednesday after Bloody Sunday.

JR: You had a kind of pub relationship with him?

SH: Yes, but closer than that term usually implies, for we had a natural, sympathetic understanding of each other. And those elegiac poems are surrounded by other elegies and by meditative poems. There is a poem called "The Badgers" which I'm very fond of—a kind of bridging of the inner and outer life. It's literally badgers, but they began in my mind to stand for the night-self, the night part in everybody, the scuttling secret parts of life. Just as in a sense the Provisionals are the night-life of the Catholic community. The skunk is a more sexual creature than the badger, and there's a poem called "The Skunk," another bit of night-life.

JR: You know the skunk in Lowell's poem?

SH: Yes, in "Skunk Hour"—but the creature I was imagining was a kindlier, slinkier one altogether.

JR: What else is in the new book?

SH: The middle of the book has some Glanmore sonnets which are really looking back on all we've been talking about. And then the last section of the book is love poems, more domestic. There are a number of elegies in it for artists too: Sean O'Riada, Robert Lowell, and an Irish poet named Francis Ledwidge who died in the First World War; and it ends up with a translation of part of Dante.

JR: You were with Lowell about a week before he died, weren't you?

SH: Yes, and for the last few years, anytime he was over in Ireland with Caroline in Castletown we met them. There was a certain trust and intimacy. He had a great gift for making you feel close, and he had tremendous grace and insight. And I felt honored by that a lot.

Recommended Books and Writers

Elegies for the Brokenhearted *by Christie Hodgen* (W. W, Norton & Company, 2010): Christie Hodgen's third book is the story of Mary Murphy and the five people in her life she will never forget. The story unfolds through the elegies of these five and their somewhat seamy lives and how they have shaped Mary into the woman she is today. Mary and her sister, Malinda are burdened with a beautiful mother who copes by running from man to man in a dying New England factory town in the 1980s. Of her mother, Mary says "Every day of your life someone crosses a room to touch you, to pinch your cheek, to stroke your hair, as if to touch you would be to take a bit of your beauty for themselves...What happens is that these people leave, in tiny smudges, traces of their desire on you, their desperation, and it spreads like a tarnish. Soon you are coated in it." Mary's story is one of inevitable abandonment but she examines her plight with a certain sorrowful wisdom and matter-of-factness. Mary's voice is unwavering in its lament and reticent survival skills. When we as readers want to scream at Mary's mother and her five marriages and scold her for continually uprooting her children, Mary's astute observations let us know that it will serve no purpose, that her mother can't help herself. As with all the characters, we are reminded that they are all doing the best they can, which is often not very good at all.

We are first introduced to Mike Beaudry, Mary's much beloved no-good uncle. "Every family had one and you were ours: the chump, the slouch, the drunk, the bum, the forever-newly-employed..." Uncle Mike lived with Mary and her sister and mother for a short while before leaving one day without a word, to never return. But while he was there he lovingly drove the girls to school each day and cared for them when their mother could not. Next we meet Elwood LePoer, a feckless classmate, "a walking joke," who Mary often empathized with, recognizing similarities in their paths or perhaps the realization that she was no better than he. It is LePoer who begrudgingly refuses to give Mary and her family a ride that introduces them to Walter Adams, a true father figure for Mary who encourages her to go to college.

Next we meet Carson Washington, Mary's college roommate. By the time Mary gets to college she has no one to write home to; her sister took off when she graduated from high school, and her mother moved south to take up with her last husband and evangelical minister she saw on late night television. It is with the death of Carson that Mary realizes she herself is drowning.

Before starting graduate school, Mary goes in search of her sister, trying desperately to reconnect. This is when she meets James Butler, a failed gay composer in the wilds of Maine, hoping that he will help her find her long lost sister. She says of James, "Throughout your childhood you waited like a customer in line at a complaint window." When Mary thinks she might just settle into a quiet albeit unproductive life in Maine, Butler gets her fired from her job and forces her hand so she'll finish graduate school.

The last ode is to her mother, Margaret Murphy Collins Francis Adams Witherspoon. This elegy is almost twice the length of the others and is often heart wrenching in the depiction of Margaret's selfishness. In this elegy, we learn of Mary's struggle for some normalcy. She is reunited with her sister briefly when her sister comes to stay with her, with her toddler, Michael, in tow. As is the way with the Sullivan family, Malinda abandons the child and Mary is left to pick up the pieces. She lives an ordinary life, back in her hometown, teaching French in the local school, trying her hardest to raise Michael in a happy, healthy environment, with no model to work from. Mary says, "What a family. Whatever instinct it was that brought families together, that bound them to one another, we lacked entirely."

Hodgen takes a risk in this collection using the second person, but her beautiful and striking prose allows her to carry off this sometimes difficult point of view. The choice of breaking this novel down into elegies is well suited for this particular point of view and the reader is rewarded in her decision.

This collection particularly spoke to me as reader as I listened to WAAF on the radio in the 1980s and was able to identify the setting through Lake Quinsigamond as Worcester, Mass. Mary Murphy discusses a French novel that she writes her graduate thesis on and in the end says, "I'd like to think that if I had written a book, it would be something like this." Throughout reading Christie Hodgen's *Elegies for the Brokenhearted*, I felt exactly the same way. —*Sarah Banse is a merit fellow at Emerson College. Her work has been published in* The Boston Globe *and* The Sun. *She is at work on her first collection of stories entitled,* Self Storage.

Selected Poems *by Mary Ruefle* (Wave Books, 2010): In his essay "Recognition, Vertigo, and Passionate Worldliness," Tony Hoagland makes sense of current divisions among poets writing in the U.S. today by dividing them into camps that go to poetry either for some sort of perspective on experience—to feel a cathartic "gong of recognition"—or to untangle their sleepy mammal selves from the probable, humdrum, and therefore mundane (Hoagland calls this "the bong of disorientation"). Mary Ruefle's *Selected Poems*, just out from Wave Books, might suggest a third alternative.

Mary Ruefle is lauded mostly for her bizarre and often surrealistic images: "She brought the tombstone home / and stood at the kitchen sink, scrubbing it," "Oh Myrtie" begins. Ruefle is also praised for her hyper-self-conscious, self-referential moves: "From my little apartment in Massachusetts / I notice and I care. God have mercy on me! / I would lie down and put a dagger in my heart / if I only knew how and where and why," one of her speakers laments. Ruefle is also praised in certain circles for finding a hundred-thousand ways of accusing "the truth" of being "just this nipple exposed beneath the rag / puce with lava-milk" and "just this beef-stink in the studio, / the popped-out eyes of rotting salmon." But Ruefle's real knack, contribution, and perhaps even obsession is her penchant for making this accusation against truth (and the possibility of meaning and meaning-making in a vicious and futile world) so playful and whimsical and hilarious that a third or new kind of truth and meaning spreads out from the oeuvre like red wine on a white tablecloth.

Many of Ruefle's poems are chunks of oratory addressed directly to the reader. This often startling breakdown of the fourth wall—"notice how I / talk to you just as if you were sitting in my lap / and not as if it

were raining, not as if there were / a sheet of water between us or anything else"—locks her meditations into an immediacy of utterance that
saves the poems from feeling too unstructured and fickle. Beyond the
irony it produces, this use of a rhetorical frame frees Ruefle's speakers to
leap wildly, sometimes across great spans of space and time: "The baby's
screams were berserk, like a bird over / the ocean, but she grew strong
and wed and left," the speaker of "Argosy" announces. This surprising
leap across the years is thrilling—it invigorates and energizes our sense
of what is possible in the world. Also, in its outlandishness, it is oddly
ferocious or headstrong and willful.

It would not be inaccurate, then, to call the speakers of Ruefle's poems authorities, even when they're muddled or uncertain, which they
rarely are: Ruefle's speakers muse in a very deliberate, declarative syntax
in a lot of universalities, generalities, and absolutes, speaking often for
all of us—"Ladies, life is no dream; Gentleman, it's a brief folly" begins
"The Pedant's Discourse" and "I tell him the whole twentieth century /
was basically a mistake" says the speaker of "Pontiac." Such generalities
create tones of great conviction, and these tones stabilize Ruefle's poems even as she undermines them, which she does at every turn, as the
imagination at work here is not only oppositional and contradictory-
-"so now I will / withdraw my interest in the whole external world /
while I am in the noticing mode" one speaker says—but primarily opposing, contradictory, contrary-to-fact, and sometimes almost hysteri-
cally dialectical, uncovering "the volatile fact / of our hidden inertia" in
one poem and "wheat and evil and insects and love" in another.

While the most obvious effect of being constantly in the midst of this
kind of up-front contrariness and hyper-hypothetical thinking—"My
mother died, / and in this fulfilled my lifelong wish to put bluebonnets
/ on a grave," says the speaker of "Pressed for Details"—is to be invigorated and awakened by surprise, sometimes something more than just
surprise happens when naked and tatted you look at the world and all
the sad and slipshod people in it from the top bucket of a Ferris Wheel
at twilight in some unnamed godforsaken country, as you do reading
Ruefle's Selected Poems.

That is, sometimes, a series of moves can add up to an utterance or ar-
ticulation that can communicate emotionally—and maybe even wisely,

as shocking as that idea might be—while disorienting and unsettling us, to return to Hoagland's formulation. I think this is really what Pound meant when he said what he said about making it new. And I think it's what most of us really want from poetry. Mary Ruefle's *Selected* collects the best and brightest from her ten books. It is way worth checking out.

—*Adrian Blevins' most recent book is* Live from the Homesick Jamboree *(Wesleyan, 2009). She teaches at Colby College in Waterville, Maine.*

Captive Voices: New and Selected Poems, 1960-2008 *by Eleanor Ross Taylor, forward by Ellen Bryant Voigt* (Louisiana State University Press, 2009): When Eleanor Ross Taylor received the Poetry Foundation's prestigious Ruth Lilly prize in 2010, Christian Wiman predicted most readers would be unfamiliar with her work. Indeed, although Taylor has been writing startlingly original, commanding poems for decades, the announcement of the prize was met in my household with "Eleanor Ross who?" Luckily, this new and selected volume should serve to introduce Taylor's poetry to the wide audience it deserves.

Presenting poems from five previous collections, as well as a generous selection of new work, *Captive Voices* shows that Taylor possesses what all good poets should have: a distinct voice that can accommodate great variation. The poems in the collection are wide-ranging—Taylor inhabits personae as diverse as Florence Nightingale and a guard on a chain gang; and her dramatic monologues, portraits, and elegies move from muscular, perfectly measured lines, such as "The battered bees hung stupid in mid-air" to free verse, like "morning mtns & / interstitial deer" and back again. Yet all are unmistakably Taylor poems, sharing the same authority, musicality, and tensions, as well as similar concerns about history, family, and place.

The title, while drawn from one of the poems, applies to the work as a whole: *Captive Voices* is populated by characters and disembodied voices, many of which speak from or against some literal or metaphorical captivity. Thus we find historical figures like Rachel Plummer, nineteenth-century prisoner of the Comanches, alongside spiritual captives, such as the artist bound by her art or the woman held captive by societal expectations. This last is a recurring theme. In "How to Live in a Trap," for example, the speaker's tongue-in-cheek instructions ("Refrain from gnawing..." "Lick wounds regularly") conclude, "Tell yourself there's a painting / in this somewhere: / Interior, Woman Singing."

With pervasive irony, inventive wordplay, and surprising metaphors (a littered hot dog carton tossed by the wind becomes "a little casket"), Taylor says a great deal in small spaces, but there is always the sense of more left unsaid, as though the poems themselves are held captive by their concise forms. (The widow of novelist Peter Taylor, Taylor began her own career writing stories but, facing the demands of motherhood and marriage, chose poetry as a less time-intensive craft.) These nuanced poems demand work on the part of the reader, requiring us to piece together back-stories and fill in details, and they yield more with every rereading.

Taylor repeatedly acknowledges her deliberate obliqueness— "Contrary to belief, the word *diary* / means undivulged; clues trail / the pages and the trail breaks off..." ("The Diary"). While the complete story is not always clear, there is a clarity of intention, a sense of the fierce intellect at work crafting the lines, choosing what to reveal. In "Long-Dreaded Event Takes Place," the speaker imagines herself a painter watching a tragedy, "pretending I recede": "everything establishes / my absence in this scene / later somewhere / I'll paint-in gaps / fill in the larger picture, / withholdings spilled / out of my pockets of resistance—." This self-imposed distance allows Taylor to capture intense emotion, whether grief or rage, with chilling precision. Consider the power and control of the lines that conclude "Where Somebody Died," when all that is left is "The brute truck / over the interstate. / The flames in the incinerator / chewing his old vests."

There's nothing new about a poet using opposing forces to create tensions (see Blake), but Taylor employs opposition to greater effect than most. She juxtaposes a plain-spoken, regional diction against coined phrases, assonance and consonance, and scattered rhymes, so that the poems strike an odd, at times disharmonious balance between artifice and natural speech. Similar tensions exist between disclosure and concealment, expansion and compression, free and metrical verse, and the narrative and lyric.

While the collection is strong from the start, Taylor's poetic craft deepens over time, and her newer poems ("newer" meaning the past

20 years or so), largely preoccupied with aging and mortality, are particularly striking. Here the personae have been largely replaced with a more personal (though still reticent) I. Possessing all of the wit, wordplay, music, and high tension of her earlier poems, these poems are more intimate and among her most resonant. Take the opening lines of "Ancestral," the final poem in the book: "Of course, we'll follow. / Did you say horse? or hearse? No matter. / They're far ahead. They started early, / shoe buckles, stovepipe hats. / / What's triter than hooves' clatter? / Is dead silence worse?" The poem goes leaping on, in love with word, sound, idea. And, of course, we follow. —*Chelsea Rathburn's poems have appeared in* Ploughshares, Poetry, *and* The Atlantic. *She is author of* The Shifting Line.

Close Calls with Nonsense: Reading New Poetry *by Stephen Burt* (Graywolf Press, 2009): It is not true, although it is sometimes ungenerously suggested, that the practitioners of contemporary poetry and its readership are one and the same set of people, but it does seem to be true that poetry reviewing is at present done mainly by poets. Since poets read more poetry and have thought harder about it than most other people, they certainly possess the basic qualifications reviewers ought to have, but too often collegiality prevails and the resulting review conveys little beyond the sparkling nothingness of a blurb. Someone's "third and most recent collection," we read, "is a complexly woven meditation— and performance—reflecting the self, its audience, and the poetic enactment of language." Yes, no doubt it is, but since so large a description might as easily fit any other poet's third, or first, or ninth collection, the would-be reader has little to go on in deciding whether to pick up this poetic enactment of language or look for another.

A rival school of collegiality-be-damned reviewing exists—e.g., the famously acerbic poet and critic William Logan—but a reflexively dismissive reviewer, while more entertaining than a reflexively flattering one, is by no means more helpful.

All the more reason, then, to be grateful for Stephen Burt. Burt is a poet, a scholar of American poetry since World War II, and arguably our most consistently readable and interesting commentator on contemporary poetry. *Close Calls with Nonsense* collects twenty-some of Burt's reviews and a few articles of more general scope into a volume that is worth reading even if one has (as I had) read several of the pieces already. Collections of a writer's previously published work have a largely deserved reputation for being diffuse and dispensable, but some such books become landmarks: Lionel Trilling's *The Liberal Imagination*, for example, and *Poetry and the Age* by Randall Jarrell. It is too soon to say whether *Close Calls with Nonsense* will have that kind of claim to posterity's attention, but there is nothing slapdash or merely opportunistic in the way it collects and organizes its diverse contents. It coheres, and an argument emerges.

Longer pieces at the beginning, middle, and end of the volume—"Close Calls with Nonsense: How to Read, and Perhaps Enjoy, Very New Poetry," "My Name is Henri: Contemporary Poets Discover John Berryman," and "The Elliptical Poets"—set out the main points of that argument. Burt usefully redescribes the familiar tradition-vs.-experimentation divide as the difference between a lyric poetry that presents itself as the voice of a relatively stable, relatively constant self with unique memories and experiences and a post-lyric poetry, influenced by continental theory's critique of the subject, which conceives of the self as a linguistic and ideological construction. Burt sees Jorie Graham's 1987 volume *The End of Beauty* as a watershed, marrying the emotional power of a distinctive personal voice to an intellectual rigor strong enough to acknowledge the fissures in selfhood and the factitiousness of language. A shoal of younger poets, Burt thinks, followed Graham's lead, some of them additionally discovering a serviceable precursor in the always fracturing, always reassembling lyric self of John Berryman's 77 *Dream Songs*. These are the writers Burt dubbed the "elliptical poets" in his best-known and most-discussed piece, first published in 1998.

Is ours the Age of the Ellipticals? Well...we'll see. The present reviewer found and finds "The Elliptical Poets" modestly persuasive, but most of the many who wrote in response took issue with the essay, sometimes in stern terms. Even so, the essay's success lies less in its persuasiveness than its having gotten a broad range of readers of poetry to engage its arguments. That an essay could, at so late a date, become a common focal point in an American poetry landscape of innumerable tribes, many of them indifferent or hostile to each other, is itself an accomplishment.

That even the "Ellipticals" themselves did not much cotton to being so known may be beside the point. After all, were the 1950s really, as Jarrell argued in a famous essay, an "Age of Criticism"? Perhaps not, but the discussion that essay inaugurated is part of the intellectual history of the United States in the 1950s.

Burt's never less than intriguing generalizations about contemporary poetry are backed up by his never less than insightful readings of individual poets. Culled from the about 150 reviews Burt has published since 1994, the pieces on individual poets are organized into three sections, one devoted to twelve mid-career contemporary U.S. poets, one to six non-U.S. Anglophone poets, and one to a kind of pantheon (Ashbery, O'Hara, Merrill, Niedecker, and five others). These reviews display again and again Burt's characteristic strengths as a critic: scholarly depth without pedantry, sophistication without recourse to jargon, intimate familiarity with the corpus and career of the poet about whom he is writing. He has an affinity for the kind of poetry he describes in "The Elliptical Poets," in which the tactics of estrangement have nonetheless an allure that draws one in, and the disintegration of the self precipitates an *aufhebung* in which we find ourselves "more truly and more strange," as Stevens put it, but he also has a gift for responding intelligently to markedly different kinds of work. The image on the book's cover, of a boy leaning back off the edge of a chair to read a book propped open upside-down on the floor, is a perfect choice, as Burt is always leaning over backward to meet a poem on its own terms. That he can write as perceptively on Richard Wilbur and Les Murray as he does on Ashbery and Denise Riley makes him the peculiarly reliable critic that he is.

Once obviously does not go to a critic with sympathies as wide as Burt's for manifestos. Fittingly, the book's last piece, "Without Evidence," is not a call to arms but a hovering cloud of aperçus, questions, and fragments. There are writers on contemporary poetry with more polemical muscle than Burt (Steve Evans, say) and those who are more explosively provocative (Kent Johnson, say), but if any place of honor remains for criticism that is undogmatic, exploratory, and written with grace and verve, Stephen Burt has first dibs on it. —*Scott Stanfield is a professor at Nebraska Wesleyan University and the lead singer and songwriter for the band Prairie Psycho.*

*Book Recommendations from
Our Advisory Editors*

Rosellen Brown recommends
*Binocular Vision: New and
Selected Stories* by Edith
Pearlman: "Elegant, deceptively
profound because their touch is
light and their prose lively and
original, these stories ought to
bring this terrific author the
attention she deserves. Many
are set in a fictional corner
of Boston called Godolphin,
where characters share space
and involvement in each
other's lives as if it were a small
town. Too many writers are
called Chekhovian, certainly,
but Pearlman's particularly
forgiving gaze—stringently
unsentimental but generous and
unjudgmental—comes as close
to deserving that epithet as any
I can think of." (Lookout Books,
January 2011)

B. H. Fairchild recommends
*Shadow: New and Selected
Poems* by Charles Harper
Webb: "Probably nobody
wants to hear again that
W. C. Fields line, 'Humor
is a serious business,' but I
find it unavoidable when
recommending Shadow Ball.
From 'The Death of Santa
Claus' to 'Kidnapper Couple
Who Forgot to Leave a Ransom
Note Sentenced to 14 Years,'
Charles Harper Webb proves
himself the funniest dead-
serious poet currently writing."
(University of Pittsburgh Press,
September 2009)

B. H. Fairchild also recommends
The Raindrop's Gospel by Maurya
Simon: "Employing a vast array
of scholarship in the service
of her own brilliant historical
imagination, Maurya Simon
offers in *The Raindrop's Gospel*
an ingenious reconstruction of
the love story of St. Jerome and
St. Paula. Simon's poetic gifts—
sensuous language, dazzling
imagery and figures, and a
variously textured lyricism—
are perfectly suited to this
extraordinary tale of love's body
and love's soul." (Elixir Press,
January 2010)

James McPherson recommends
Gold Boy, Emerald Girl: Stories
by Yiyun Li: "Ms. Li is an
excellent young writer who has
just been awarded a MacArthur
Fellowship. I worked with her
some years ago, before and after

she enrolled in the Iowa Writers' Workshop." (Random House, September 2010)

Maura Stanton recommends *Portraits of a Few of the People I've Made Cry: Stories* by Christine Sneed: "This book of stories, winner of The Grace Paley Prize in Short Fiction from AWP, contains ten mesmerizing stories about nurses, screenwriters, teachers, movie stars, painters, bookkeepers, and hairdressers—ordinary and extraordinary people struggling for what we all struggle for— love, connection, and the recognition that our lives matter." (University of Massachusetts Press, November 2010)

EDITORS' CORNER
New Books by Our Advisory Editors

Charles Baxter, *Gryphon: New and Selected Stories*, fiction (Pantheon, January 2011)

Ann Beattie, *The New Yorker Stories*, fiction (Scribner, November 2010)

B. H. Fairchild, *Beauty*, poetry (Blackbird Press)

David Gullette, *The Genealogical Construction of the Kyrgyz Republic*, non-fiction (University of Cambridge, September 2010)

Gish Jen, *World and Town*, a novel (Knopf, October 2010)

Antonya Nelson, *Bound: A Novel*, fiction (Bloomsbury USA, September 2010)

Carl Phillips, *Double Shadow*, poetry (Farrar, Strauss and Giroux, April 2011)

Jim Shepard, *You Think That's Bad: Stories*, short stories (Knopf, March 2011)

C. D. Wright, *One With Others*, poetry and prose (Copper Canyon Press, November 2010)

Kevin Young, *Ardency: A Chronicle of the Amistad Rebels*, poetry (Knopf, February 2011)

Rabih Alameddine has written three novels, *The Hakawati* (Anchor Books), *I, the Divine* (W. W. Norton & Company), and *Koolaids* (Picador), and a book of short stories, *The Perv* (Picador).

John Bargowski has new work scheduled to appear in *Prairie Schooner, Poetry Northwest, Journal of New Jersey Poets,* and *The Sun.* He is the recipient of a 2009 National Endowment for the Arts Fellowship, a New Jersey State Council on the Arts Distinguished Artist Fellowship, and the Theodore Roethke Prize.

David Blair grew up in Pittsburgh. His first book, *Ascension Days* (Del Sol Press), was chosen by Thomas Lux for the Del Sol Press Poetry Prize. Blair is an associate professor at The New England Institute of Art.

Eavan Boland's most recent book is *New Collected Poems* (W. W. Norton & Company). A book of prose is coming out in spring 2011 with W. W. Norton called *A Journey with Two Maps.* Boland teaches at Stanford University.

Bruce Bond's most recent collections of poetry include *The Visible* (LSU, forthcoming), *Peal* (Etruscan, 2009), and *Blind Rain* (Finalist, The Poet's Prize, LSU, 2008). His poetry has appeared in *Best American Poetry, The Southern Review, The Virginia Quarterly Review, The Georgia Review, The New Republic, The Gettysburg Review,* and many other journals. Presently he is a Regents Professor of English at the University of North Texas and Poetry Editor for *American Literary Review.*

Catherine Carter was born in Maryland and now lives, with her husband, in Cullowhee near Western Carolina University, where she coordinates the English education program. Her first collection, *The Memory of Gills* (LSU Press), received the 2007 Roanoke-Chowan Award from the North Carolina Literary and Historical Association. Her work has also appeared or is forthcoming in *Poetry, Orion,* and *The Best American Poetry 2009,* among other publications. Her next volume of poetry, *The Swamp Monster at Home,* is forthcoming from LSU Press in spring 2012.

Harry Clifton was born in Dublin in 1952 but has lived in Africa and Asia, as well as, more recently, in Europe. He has published six collections of poems, including *The Desert Route: Selected Poems 1973-1988* (Gallery Press, 1992) and *Secular Eden: Paris Notebooks 1994-2004* (Wake Forest University Press, 2007). *On the Spine of Italy,* his prose study of an Abruzzese mountain community, was published by Macmillan in 1999. For ten years he lived in France, publishing *Le Canto d'Ulysse,* his poems in French translation, in 1996. He returned to Ireland in 2004 and lives in Dublin, where he is currently Ireland Professor of Poetry.

Nicole Cullen was raised in Salmon, Idaho. She is an MFA candidate and a James A. Michener Fellow at The University of Texas at Austin.

Michael Dickman was born and raised in Portland, Ore. He is the author of *The End of the West* and *Flies* (both published by Copper Canyon Press).

Gerard Fanning was born in Dublin in 1952. He is a graduate of University College Dublin. His awards include the Rooney Prize for Irish Literature and bursaries from the Arts Council of Ireland. *Hombre: New & Selected Poems* is due from Dedalus Press this year.

Gary Fincke's most recent collection, *The History of Permanence,* won the 2010 Stephen F. Austin University Press Poetry Prize and will be published in 2011. Michigan State University Press published his memoir, *The Canals of Mars,* in 2010. He is the Charles B. Degenstein Professor of Creative Writing at Susquehanna University.

Tessa Hadley's fourth novel, *The London Train,* will be out in the U.S. in June 2011, with Harper Collins. Her short stories are published regularly in *The New Yorker* and *Granta,* and she reviews for *London Review of Books.* She teaches literature and creative writing at Bath Spa University.

Rita Ann Higgins published her first five collections of poetry with Salmon Poetry. Bloodaxe Books published her next three, including *Throw in the Vowels: New and Selected Poems,* which was reissued in 2010 with an audio CD. In 2010, Salmon Poetry published *Hurting God: Part Essay, Part Rhyme,* and in 2011, Bloodaxe Books will publish her new collection.

Ewa Hryniewicz-Yarbrough is a translator and essayist. She has translated two novels from Polish: *Annihilation* (Dalkey Archive Press) and *Rat* (Arcade Publishing). Her most recent book of translation is *They Carry a Promise,* a collection of poems by Janusz Szuber (Knopf). Her essays have appeared in *The American Scholar, TriQuarterly, The Threepenny Review* and the *San Francisco Chronicle.* A native of Poland, she lives north of Boston.

Jonathan Johnson is the author of two books of poems, *Masodon, 80% Complete* and *In the Land We Imagined Ourselves* (both from Carnegie Melon University Press), and the nonfiction book *Hannah and the Mountain: Notes Toward a Wilderness Fatherhood* (University of Nebraska Press). Johnson migrates between upper Michigan, Scotland, and eastern Washington, where he teaches in the MFA program at Eastern Washington University.

Hester Kaplan is the author of *The Edge of Marriage* (University of Georgia Press), winner of the Flannery O'Connor Award for Short Fiction, and *Kinship Theory.* Her stories have appeared in *The Best American Short Stories,* and this is her third appearance in *Ploughshares.* She teaches in Lesley University's MFA Program in Creative Writing.

Peter Kline's poems have appeared in *Poetry, Tin House* magazine, *Crazyhorse, Crab Orchard Review,* and elsewhere. He has been honored with the 2010 Morton Marr Poetry Prize from *Southwest Review* and a Wallace Stegner Fellowship from Stanford University, where he is currently the William Chace Lecturer in Creative Nonfiction.

Nick Laird was born in County Tyrone in 1975, and has published four books, of which the most recent are *Glover's Mistake* (Viking), a novel, and *On Purpose* (W. W. Norton & Company), a collection of poems. He has won many awards for his work, including the Geoffrey Faber Memorial Prize, the Rooney Prize, and the Ireland Chair of Poetry Award.

Shaena Lambert's stories have appeared recently in *Zoetrope: All Story* and *Best Canadian Stories* 2010 and 2011. Her novel *Radiance* (Random House) was a *Globe and Mail* best book and a finalist for the Writers' Trust award. Her collection *The Falling Woman* (Vintage) was published to acclaim in Canada, the U.K., and Germany. She lives in Vancouver.

Cleopatra Mathis' seventh book of poems, *Book of Dog*, will be published by Sarabande in late 2012. She teaches at Dartmouth College, where she is the Frederick Sessions Beebe Professor in the Art of Writing.

Michael Morse has poems forthcoming in *The American Poetry Review* and *The Lumberyard*. His poems have appeared in the anthologies *Broken Land: Poems of Brooklyn* and *Starting Today: 100 Poems for Obama's First 100 Days*. He lives in New York City and teaches at Ethical Culture Fieldston School.

Paul Muldoon's main collections of poetry are *New Weather* (Faber & Faber), *Mules, Why Brownlee Left, Quoof,* and *Meet-*

ing the British (Wake Forest University Press and Faber & Faber); *Madoc: A Mystery, The Annals of Chile, Hay, Poems 1968-1998, Moy Sand and Gravel, Horse Latitudes,* and *Maggot* (Faber & Faber and Farrar, Straus and Giroux).

Mary O'Malley was born and raised in Connemara. She has published six collections of poetry and her seventh, titled *Valparaiso* is due out from Carcanet in May 2012. She taught for several years at the New University of Lisbon in Portugal and lectured in poetry on the MA in writing, as well as in arts education at University College Galway for many years. She has received awards for her poems, including a Hennessey Award and the Lawrence O'Shaughnessey Award for poetry in the U.S. O'Malley also writes for radio and is a regular broadcaster. She has taught and lectured and read her work throughout Europe and the U.S. and is currently at work on a memoir of place.

Don Paterson works as a musician and editor, and lectures at the University of St Andrews, Scotland. His most recent collection of poetry is *Rain* (FSG,

2010), which was awarded the 2010 Forward Prize for Best Collection in the U.K.

Angela Pneuman's collection of stories, *Home Remedies,* was published by Harcourt in 2007. Her fiction has appeared in *The Best American Short Stories, New England Review, The Iowa Review, The Virginia Quarterly Review,* and previously in *Ploughshares.* She lives in Napa Valley, Calif., and is hard at work on a novel.

Sam Sullivan is a graduate of Saint Ann's School and is currently a sophomore at Yale University. He grew up in Portland, Ore., and Brooklyn, N.Y., and has written no books. His poems have appeared in *Hanging Loose* magazine.

Lynne Tillman is a novelist, short story writer, and essayist. Her most recent novel is *American Genius, A Comedy* (Soft Skull Press), the subject of a casebook on Electronic Book Review. Her fourth collection of short stories, *Someday This Will Be Funny* (Red Lemonade), will appear in late April 2011.

Ryan Vine's manuscript, *Shiv,* was a finalist for the 2009 May Swenson Poetry Award. He has won a Weldon Kees Award from Backwaters Press and the Robert Watson Poetry Prize from *The Greensboro Review.* He has recent work in *The American Poetry Review,* and his criticism appears regularly in the Minneapolis *Star Tribune.* Ryan received his MFA from Emerson College and teaches at the College of St. Scholastica in Duluth, Minn.

CK Williams' most recent book of poems, *Wait* (Farrar, Straus and Giroux), was published in 2010, as was a prose study, *On Whitman* (Princeton University Press), and a children's book, *A Not Scary Story About Big Scary Things* (Harcourt Children's Press). He is a member of the American Academy of Arts and Letters and teaches in the Program in Creative Writing at Princeton University.

GUEST EDITOR POLICY

Ploughshares is published three times a year: mixed issues of poetry and prose in the spring and winter and a prose issue in the fall, with each guest-edited by a different writer of prominence. Guest editors are invited to solicit up to half of their issues, with the other half selected from unsolicited manuscripts screened for them by staff editors. This guest editor policy is designed to introduce readers to different literary circles and tastes, and to offer a fuller representation of the range and diversity of contemporary letters than would be possible with a single editorship. Yet, at the same time, we expect every issue to reflect our overall standards of literary excellence.

SUBMISSION POLICIES

Please note that our reading period has changed, effective June 2010. We welcome unsolicited manuscripts from June 1 to January 15 (postmark dates). All submissions postmarked from January 16 to May 31 will be returned unread. Submit your work at any time during our reading period; if a manuscript is not timely for one issue, it will be considered for another. We do not recommend trying to target specific guest editors. Our backlog is unpredictable, and staff editors ultimately have the responsibility of determining for which editor a work is most appropriate. We accept submissions online. Please see our Web site (www.pshares.org) for more information and specific guidelines. Unsolicited work sent directly to a guest editor's home or office will be ignored and discarded; guest editors are formally instructed not to read such work. All mailed manuscripts and correspondence regarding submissions should be accompanied by a self-addressed, stamped envelope (s.a.s.e.). Manuscript copies will be recycled, not returned. No replies will be given by e-mail (exceptions are made for international submissions). Expect three to five months for a decision. We now receive well over a thousand manuscripts a month. Do not query us until five months have passed, and if you do, please write to us, including an s.a.s.e. and indicating the postmark date of submission. Simultaneous submissions are amenable as long as they are indicated as such and we are notified immediately upon acceptance elsewhere. We cannot accommodate revisions, changes of return address, or forgotten s.a.s.e.'s after the fact. We do not reprint previously published work. Translations are welcome if permission has been granted. We cannot be responsible for delay, loss, or damage. Payment is upon publication: $25/printed page, $50 minimum and $250 maximum per author, with two copies of the issue and a one-year subscription.

Dorothy Sargent Rosenberg Annual Poetry Prizes, 2011

Prize winners for the 2010 competition, announced February 5, 2011

$7,500 prizes to Lisa Ampleman, Kimi Cunningham Grant, Éireann Lorsung and Bruce Snider

$5,000 prizes to Paula Bohince, Rachel Dilworth, Tarfia Faizullah, Brieghan Gardner, Eric Leigh, Debbie Lim, Angie K. Mazakis, Claire McQuerry, Emily Louise Smith, Jennifer K. Sweeney and Mark Wagenaar

$2,500 prizes to Scott Cameron, Dan Disney, Ari Finkelstein, Jules Gibbs, Brian Patrick Heston, Maria Hummel, Charles Jensen, Andrew Krewer, Nina Lindsay, Susan L. Miller, Rebecca Parson, Rachel Richardson, Sarah Sousa, Sarah Sweeney, Matthew Thorburn and Jessica Young

$1,000 prizes to Marla Alupoaicei, Melissa Barrett, Lindsay Bernal, Charles Byrne, Chuck Carlise, Tom Christopher, Austin L. Church, Chanda Feldman, Michael J. Grabell, K.A. Hays, Wesley Holtermann, Tess Jolly, Jenn Koiter, Gary L. McDowell, Christopher Nelson, Joanna Pearson, Melissa Range and Michael Rutherglen

There were also thirteen Honorable Mentions at $250 each

Thank you to everyone who entered and congratulations to our winners

We now happily announce our 2011 competition

Prizes ranging from $1,000 up to as much as $25,000 will be awarded for the finest lyric poems celebrating the human spirit. The contest is open to all writers, published or unpublished, who will be under the age of 40 on November 6, 2011. Entries must be postmarked on or before the third Saturday in October (October 15, 2011). Only previously unpublished poems are eligible for prizes. Names of prize winners will be published on our website on February 5, 2012, together with a selection of the winning poems. Please visit our website www.DorothyPrizes.org for further information and to read poems by previous winners.

Checklist of Contest Guidelines
• Entries must be postmarked on or before October 15, 2011.
• Past winners may re-enter until their prizes total in excess of $25,000.
• All entrants must be under the age of 40 on November 6, 2011.
• Submissions must be original, previously unpublished, and in English: no translations, please.
• Each entrant may submit one to three separate poems.
• Only one of the poems may be more than thirty lines in length.
• Each poem must be printed on a separate sheet.
• Submit two copies of each entry with your name, address, phone number and email address clearly marked on each page of one copy only.
• Include an index card with your name, address, phone number and email address and the titles of each of your submitted poems.
• Include a $10 entry fee payable to the Dorothy Sargent Rosenberg Memorial Fund. (This fee is not required for entrants resident outside the U.S.A.)
• Poems will not be returned. Include a stamped addressed envelope if you wish us to acknowledge receipt of your entry.

Mail entries to:
Dorothy Sargent Rosenberg Poetry Prizes, PO Box 2306, Orinda, California 94563.

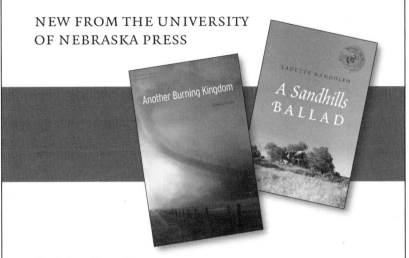

"If a nation loses its storytellers, it loses its childhood." —Peter Handke

Michener Center for Writers
MFA in WRITING
FICTION   POETRY   SCREENWRITING   PLAYWRITING

A top ranked program. Dedicated and diverse resident faculty. Inspiring and distinguished visiting writers. $25,000 annual fellowships. Three years in Austin, Texas.

www.utexas.edu/academic/mcw
512-471-1601

THE UNIVERSITY OF TEXAS AT AUSTIN

$15,000 in Awards

21st Annual Jeffrey E. Smith

EDITORS' PRIZE

$5,000 Fiction • $5,000 Poetry • $5,000 Essay

The Missouri Review is now accepting submissions for the 21st Annual Jeffrey E. Smith Editors' Prize competition.

In addition to the $15,000 awarded to the first place winners, three finalists in each category receive cash awards and are considered for publication. Past winners have been reprinted in the *Best American* series.

Page Restrictions

Fiction and nonfiction entries should not exceed 25 typed, double-spaced pages. Poetry entries can include any number of poems up to 10 pages in total. Each story, essay, or group of poems constitutes one entry.

Entry Fee

$20 for each entry (checks made payable to *The Missouri Review*). Each fee includes a one-year subscription (digital or print!) to *TMR*. Please enclose a complete e-mail and mailing address.

Entry Instructions

Include the printable contest entry form (available online). On the first page of each submission, include author's name, address, e-mail and telephone number. Entries must be previously unpublished and will not be returned. Mark the outside of the envelope "Fiction," "Essay," or "Poetry." Each entry in a separate category must be mailed in a separate envelope. Enclose a #10 SASE or e-mail address for an announcement of winners.

Go Green: Enter Online!

We are also accepting electronic submissions. For details, go to *www.missourireview.com/contest*

Mailing Address

Missouri Review Editors' Prize
357 McReynolds Hall
University of Missouri
Columbia, MO 65211

The Missouri Review

Postmark Deadline October 1, 2011

www.mississippireview.com

PLOUGHSHARES

Stories and poems for literary afficionados

Known for its compelling fiction and poetry, *Ploughshares* is widely regarded as one of America's most influential literary journals. Each issue is guest-edited by a different writer for a fresh, provocative slant—exploring personal visions, aesthetics, and literary circles—and contributors include both well-known and emerging writers. *Ploughshares* has become a premier proving ground for new talent, showcasing the early works of Sue Miller, Mona Simpson, Robert Pinsky, Tim O'Brien, and countless others. Past guest editors include Richard Ford, Derek Walcott, Tobias Wolff, Kathryn Harrison, and Lorrie Moore. This unique editorial format has made *Ploughshares* a dynamic anthology series—one that has established a tradition of quality and prescience. *Ploughshares* is published in April, August, and December, usually with a prose issue in the fall and mixed issues of poetry and fiction in the spring and winter. Inside each issue, you'll find not only great new stories and poems, but also a profile on the guest editor, book reviews, and miscellaneous notes about *Ploughshares*, its writers, and the literary world. Subscribe today.

Subscribe online at www.pshares.org.

☐ Send me a one-year subscription for $30.
  I save $12 off the cover price (3 issues).

☐ Send me a two-year subscription for $50.
  I save $34 off the cover price (6 issues).

Start with: ☐ Spring ☐ Fall ☐ Winter

Name _____

Address _____

_____

E-mail _____

Mail with check to: Ploughshares • Emerson College
      120 Boylston St. • Boston, MA 02116

Add $12 per year for international postage ($10 for Canada).